Why a Suffering
World Makes Sense

Why a Suffering World Makes Sense

Chris Tiegreen

BakerBooks
Grand Rapids, Michigan

Published by Baker Books
a division of Baker Publishing Group
P.O. Box 6287, Grand Rapids, MI 49516-6287
www.bakerbooks.com

Printed in the United States of America

Library of Congress Cataloging-in-Publication Data
Tiegreen, Chris.
    Why a suffering world makes sense / Chris Tiegreen.
        p.   cm.
    Includes bibliographical references.
    ISBN 0-8010-6575-5 (pbk.)
    1. Theodicy. 2. Consolation. 3. Suffering—Religious aspects—Christian-
ity. I. Title.
BT160.T54 2006
231'.8—dc22   2005020422

Published in association with the literary agency of Mark Sweeney & Associates,
28540 Altessa Way, Suite 201, Bonita Springs, FL 34135.

To my three sons, Christopher, Jonathan, and Timothy. You know the pain of this world in ways a father wishes you never had to experience. May you one day know glory in ways a father can scarcely imagine now.

Contents

Contents

Foreword

Why a Suffering World Makes Sense may seem like a crazy title to some people. "Sense" is not what most people see when they look at the troubles of this world. When hardship comes, we may wonder why we have it, and we may pray for relief, but we usually fall short of explanations. A suffering world doesn't offer us many answers.

But in this case, *Why a Suffering World Makes Sense* is not only an excellent title but an excellent book. Chris Tiegreen is a colleague and award-winning writer for Walk Thru the Bible, and it is my privilege to have the opportunity to serve in ministry with him. Chris writes not as someone who has studied the problem of suffering from an office but as someone who has lived through it and wrestled with its implications. You won't find complete answers in this book, but you will find answers, and they aren't what you might expect. While many people despair and grow bitter from their trials, Chris insists that the Bible has some surprising angles on suffering that few people notice. God has good purposes for us—and good purposes for his own glory—that we have barely begun to grasp.

9

If you have struggled with the age-old issue of how a good God and a suffering world go hand in hand, then you will likely be encouraged by this fresh look at an old topic. You will not simply find theological concepts and old arguments about the issue of suffering and the goodness of God, but you will find fresh insight from someone who has been there and shows us the way as God has shown him.

Chip Ingram, president of Walk Thru the Bible,
teaching pastor of *Living on the Edge* radio program

Acknowledgments

Writing a book usually doesn't scare me. I actually enjoy the process of spilling my guts onto paper. But sharing the results with a large audience? That's terrifying.

So my first step is always to share the results with a small and safe audience, readers who, if they must challenge the results, will do so gently and with large doses of encouragement. I am truly grateful for the feedback, suggestions, support, and all-around generosity of those who read this manuscript and offered their opinions: the publishing/editorial team at Walk Thru the Bible, especially Jim Gabrielsen, Paula Kirk, Scott Woods, Laurin Makohon, and Tim Walker; our ministry's president and most enthusiastic cheerleader, Chip Ingram; my pastor, Scot Sherman; fellow writer Mary Zimnik; and last but not least, my editor at Baker, Vicki Crumpton. Thank you all for your input.

And, of course, I am deeply indebted to my wife, Hannah, who tolerates the late hours of the writing process quite well, and who offers precious encouragement not only for writing but also for life in this world.

Introduction

Wandering the Wastelands

The whole world lies in the power of the evil one.

1 John 5:19 NASB

Eden's gone. It was our playground and our sanctuary all rolled into one. There we met with God; he was no distant deity in our minds, but a companion. There we tended the land, but everything was abundantly supplied. No one died there. No one even got hurt there. There was no decay, no sorrow, no pain. But it's gone.

You don't remember it, do you? Neither do I. We know about it because it's in the first pages of our Scriptures. But if neither our memory nor our Scriptures gave us any clues about the garden, we would still long for it. It's buried deep in our psyches, written somewhere in our genetics, and lingering in our desires. We try to reconstruct it here in the wastelands we now wander, but it remains elusive. It's a haunting call from a forgotten past, and we miss it.

The wind howls and the sun scorches in these wastelands we now wander. Some of us crave an oasis to pitch our tent in; others long for a cave to hide in. We live between the Garden of Eden and the City of God, and we ask a lot of questions about why we're here. Being here hurts. With Eden behind us and heaven ahead, we want to know the purpose of the interim. You ask questions about it, and so do I.

That's what the pages that follow are about. These are the answers I've found in my search of the Scriptures and my struggles with pain. Some theologians have suggested these answers—the subject has been discussed so much that there are few, if any, new ideas left—but I've never heard or read a thoroughly developed treatment from the angle I'm about to take. I'm not sure why. Perhaps these musings are too basic, already common knowledge to greater minds. There are certainly deep thinkers out there who are better qualified to put forth a formal apologetic on the problem of evil. Many of them have, so that's not my purpose here; this book is better seen as a somewhat ordered series of meditations on a subject common to all of us. I have a hunch that many people will see the premise of this book as shallow; it offers answers, and that's not a popular thing to do when discussing the problem of evil. But I believe these answers deeply. They aren't complete, but they help me hang on to a sense of sanity and purpose.

Maybe this book will help you as you wonder why Eden is so far behind and heaven is so far ahead. I think the Bible gives us the reason for the pain, the answer to the problem of evil, the purpose of the barren wastelands where you and I now dwell—even a promise to hold on to while we're here. Our suffering has confused us, and we've all asked God lots of whys. His answer, I believe, is a really, really good one.

PART 1

THE **PAIN**

*The whole creation has been groaning together in the pains
of childbirth until now.*

Romans 8:22

1

Something's Wrong

In the world you will have tribulation.

John 16:33

I remember the first time I saw death. It was sometime in the late '60s, when I was five or six years old. There were two men on a TV news clip, one with a gun and one bound as a prisoner. One of them was Vietcong; the other was a member of the resistance. I forget which was which, and it doesn't really matter. What sticks in my memory is the moment when the man with the gun suddenly lifted it and shot the prisoner in the head. The victim immediately fell to the ground. I was stunned. I knew people died, but I'd never seen it happen. One moment the man was standing there alive, and the next moment he was a motionless corpse. Alive. Then dead. All in less than a second.

I tried to imagine what it was like to be him. Did he know he was breathing his last breath? Was he afraid? Where was he after he died? Heaven? Hell? Nonexistent? Was he standing before God explaining why he had never heard the gospel or, if he had, why he'd never accepted it? Was he in utter, black unconsciousness, just another meaningless victim of a random, nihilist universe? Five-year-olds don't know how to verbalize those questions. But when confronted with the crisis of mortality, they think them somewhere deep down inside their little souls. I certainly did.

I also tried to imagine what it was like to be the man with the gun. Was that hard for him to do? Didn't look like it. Was his heart filled with hate, or was he just ignorant about the implications of his actions? Did he understand the feelings of his victim, or was he an unfeeling killing machine? What drove him to such callousness? Orders from his superiors? Personal vengeance? Why was this so routine for him and so traumatic for me? Was he really as casual about homicide as he appeared? I don't know. I can't know. I wasn't there, and I don't expect I'll ever be in a similar situation.

But I will die. That transition from life to death will happen for me as it has for billions of souls throughout human history. That knowledge sank into the core of my heart as I tried to process that horrific image.

The question we all ask was stuck in my mind from that moment on. It would have happened sooner or later; there was nothing particularly unique about my first exposure to death. The question would have been forced on me one day if it had not been forced on me right then. The image of death is too inescapable, and the question is universal. Five-year-olds ask it when it first occurs to them, and they continue to ask it when they're ninety-five-year-olds. It plagues us. From the moment we realize we live in a shattered world, in the back of our minds is this question: why?

Almost every religion attempts to answer this question. Mine certainly does. But regardless of our religious worldview, we can't be definitive about the answers. We can speculate, and we can propose reasons, and, to a degree, we can even explain how evil came into this world. After all, many of us believe we have God's authoritative revelation, don't we? It certainly has something to say about this problem; if it didn't, it wouldn't come from a very relevant God. But the why behind the how, the ultimate explanation of evil, continues to elude us. Even so, we just can't drop the question. Some people do a good job of ignoring it and deciding that, as far as they're concerned, it doesn't matter. But they're fooling themselves. It's still there.

I'm not very good at ignoring it, so I continue to ask it. I asked it throughout the rest of the '60s as I heard reports of massacres and riots. It was in the back of my mind when my mother made us stay in the basement one afternoon, afraid of what might erupt in the streets of Atlanta as the news of Martin Luther King Jr.'s assassination spread. It weighed on my heart every time I saw the film clip of JFK slumping down in the back of the limo while Jackie frantically tried to climb out.

The years since have done nothing to convince me that the question isn't legitimate. The killing fields, the White House scandals, the drugs at school, the guns at school, the people who show me their most offensive finger after they've cut me off in traffic, the friends who have died while I have been allowed to live, the social problems of a secular culture, the things I say when I stub my toe, the persistence of this thing we call sin—all of it nags at us with the fact that the question is forever legitimate and the answer is forever elusive. Or so it seems.

About the time I first sat down to write some of these thoughts, terrorists decided that my country was so abhorrent that they were justified in killing thousands of people by destroying two commercial towers. Our country was thrust into war, and our illusion of security was shattered. Two months later my sixteen-year-old son was in a car accident that left him comatose for nearly six weeks. The question was there as I sat by his bedside, hearing news reports about the war on terror and waiting for the doctor to tell me whether his prediction du jour was for life or for death; and it has remained as I've watched a once hopeful young man deal with severe limitations and frustrations that may—if some doctors who know a lot about brain injuries are correct—plague him the rest of his life.

These are two of my traumas, one of which you probably share and the other of which you can probably relate to. My story isn't unique. It's not even unusual. If you've lived any time at all in this world, you've experienced pain. You've seen people suffer, and you've seen people die. You've been offended, and you've been guilty of offenses. You've cried yourself to sleep, and you've made others cry. Though you strive to escape the threat of evil, you know that as long as you dwell on this broken planet, you never will.

It Hurts Here

There is no denying that evil is in this world. Bad things happen, people commit blatant sins, blood is shed, corruption runs rampant, truth is dismissed as relative, babies are killed, children are abused, diseases are epidemic, weapons proliferate, wars are rumored, bombers commit suicide and homicide all in the same misguided explosion of passion and pain, lonely teenagers jump from buildings, and people who say they love each other don't. I will never understand those who can read the headlines every day and then assert that people are basically good. I will never understand those who believe that spiritual problems can be solved with social programs, that peace can be achieved by treaties, that prejudices can be eliminated by discussion, that rebellious youth can be corrected with heavy doses of esteem and understanding, that scars can be healed through therapy, that wrongs can be righted by litigation, and that diseases can be eliminated by research. Evil is woven into the fabric of humanity, and it's obvious.

I've got no complaint against any of our feeble attempts at solving these massive problems, but the issue is surely too deep to be resolved by positive thinking, human ingenuity, and cooperative efforts. Education won't do it, and neither will politics, economic reform, social programs, or any other can-do, we-can-solve-all-our-problems-together approach. Our problem—this global problem of evil and sin and suffering—runs through and through, all the way down to the core of every human heart. It is universal. It is unyielding. And, in spite of all the efforts through all the ages to arrive at some semblance of utopia, it seems to be getting worse.

I have to ask why. You do too. The circumstances that brought that question to your mind are likely different from mine, but the thought is the same. You've noticed the problem, and you've wrestled with the reason it is there. You and I both know that philosophers and theologians have found the existence of evil plus the existence of God more than a little troubling. They have also found the existence of evil plus the theoretical nonexistence of God utterly depressing. The political, economic, and social systems that have approached life with this latter perspective have failed to improve the human condition at all and have devastated the human psyche in their attempts. So we go back to the former approach, as troubling as it is. We were built for hope, and we have to hang on to it. We were also built for understanding, so we must continue to ask our questions. Acknowledging the pain and trying to move on with life just isn't possible for us. We have to explore the reasons behind it.

The pages that follow are one more effort among many to do that. There have been plenty of attempts at an explanation, some of them quite perceptive and some of them far too superficial. Some of them satisfy us a little, others help us hang on until we can get the answers one day in some future enlightened state, and others just offer comfort while we hurt. Any answer that would be meaningful to a Christian has to be drawn straight from the Bible. We who believe in the hope of the gospel of Jesus Christ must begin with what our tradition and our Scriptures have told us. That is where our struggle begins.

Theology's Tightest Knot

"So how can you reconcile the existence of suffering with a God who cares?" my classmate John asked me as we waited for the campus bus. We had just come out of an introductory seminar in religious studies, a class that to that point in the semester had disappointed me. I had recently become interested in learning more about the God of Christianity and had already wrestled with whether I thought the Bible was his revealed Word or not. I was firm in my conviction that it was, and I had enthusiastically signed up for this class, expecting to learn more about the Bible itself. Lectures about theologians, heavy on nineteenth-century German liberalism, were not what I had in mind. So when the question of the problem of evil came up, I was already impatient with critiques of Christianity. The issue was already resolved in my thinking, not from any intellectual understanding of how the attributes of God applied to it, but from a simple acceptance of God's Word. The Bible teaches that God is sovereign and that he is love, in spite of clear evidence of rampant evil and excruciating suffering in this world.

Still, I had no answer for John other than "This is what the Bible says." The issue had not been explored enough for him in class, and he wanted to discuss it further, especially with someone who believed the apparently contradictory suppositions taught by the Bible. He wanted to know how God's alleged Word resolved the obvious conflict. And though the integrity of revelation seemed at stake in my answer, all I could do was say, "The Bible doesn't resolve it, as far as I know. It just holds these truths and lets them remain in tension." It wasn't a satisfying answer to John, and, deep down, it wasn't satisfying to me either. My bus came, and I got on it while he remained to wait for his. *Conversation over*, I said to myself with a sigh of relief. I was spared from hearing accusations that my faith was anti-intellectual, a naive acceptance of things that don't make sense.

This certainly wasn't the first time I'd been confronted with the issue of evil, having heard high school teachers and philosophy lecturers point to it as a flaw in the Christian worldview. And it by no means was the last time I'd have to deal with it either—seminary professors, church members, and skeptics of the faith have raised it repeatedly in the years since college. It is one of those problems—perhaps the main one—that atheists use to rationalize their belief in the nonexistence of God. Both at an intellectual level in theoretical discussion and at a personal level in the middle of a crisis, the problem seems to undermine the existence of a good creator. History is full of people who could never reconcile this world and our God. My friend John was not alone in his questions.

Even Christian theologians acknowledge the lack of tidy answers to the problem; there are none. John Stott calls the fact of suffering "the single greatest challenge to the Christian faith."[1] Lee Strobel lists it as objection number one among the issues he addresses in his recent book *The Case for Faith*.[2] Any decent Christian apologetic gives prominence to the problem. Evangelism courses almost always include a brief rebuttal for trainees to learn for those times when a seeker raises the question. Why? Because seekers almost always raise the question. And while I'd always dismissed it as just one of those things God doesn't answer for us, I knew at some level that there had to be more evidence in the Bible than what I'd already discerned. I just hadn't found it yet.

I have a couple of books of famous quotations from Christian writers and speakers. A quick look at the entry "evil" in either of them reveals how pervasive the question is. "The problem of evil is one of the most crucial protests raised by unbelievers against the fact of God," said James Orr. "Evil constitutes the biggest single argument against the existence of an almighty, loving God," said John W. Wenham. "All simplifications of religious dogma are shipwrecked upon the rock of the problem of evil," said A. N. Whitehead. These three are merely a small, random sampling. There are more. Many, many more. Nearly every theological thinker has a quote about the question.

Long ago the Greek philosopher Epicurus put it this way:

> Either God wants to abolish evil, and cannot;
> or he can, but does not want to;
> or he cannot and does not want to.
> If he wants to, but cannot, he is impotent.

If he can, and does not want to, he is wicked.
But, if God both can and wants to abolish evil,
then how comes evil in the world?[3]

He posed three things commonly held to be true and decided that all three—God's goodness, God's power, and the existence of evil—could not coexist. Because they couldn't coexist, and because the existence of evil was obvious and therefore nonnegotiable, Epicurus was convinced that God had to be either compromised or denied altogether. Many others throughout history—multitudes, in fact—have been convinced of the same conclusion.

Though most Christians would argue that the goodness and power of God are both quite demonstrable and concrete, they are less visible to the eyes of this world. We can say that his goodness and power are nonnegotiable, and according to the revelation we so strongly believe, they are. We can't prove them to a skeptic or a seeker, however, so they make easy targets. But no one approaches this conundrum by trying to undermine the third proposition: the existence of evil. For people who frame the problem the way Epicurus did, the proposition always compromised is one of the characteristics of God. Evil is simply too obvious.

What about the Holocaust?

The question in the twentieth century commonly took the form of current events: Where was God during the Holocaust? for example. I recently read a story of a concentration camp survivor whose guards buried him up to his neck in the ground. After having his head kicked like a soccer ball for the guards' entertainment, he was forced to watch as his wife was shot in the head and killed. Then he observed an even worse horror: his infant daughter was tossed in the air and caught on a guard's bayonet. He watched her writhe and die on the sharp end of a gun. The man buried in the ground survived, if you can call a life with those kinds of memories survival.[4]

Indeed, where was God? That story, better than any philosophical construct, puts the question in its ugliest, most nauseating terms—and ultimately in its most real and relevant terms. Why was there a holocaust in which six million Jews died or Soviet gulags in which many more millions of political dissidents and Christian believers died? Why are there world wars and never-ending regional conflicts? Why have there been genocides and pogroms and famines and epidemics and suffering to the degree that pretechnological peoples could scarcely imagine? Or, at a more individual level, why do couples get divorced and friends commit suicide? The world in which these sorts of things happen is not a hypothetical one. The question of pain is not an abstract with which we wrestle. It's deep and personal, and it means everything to us. We don't seek an answer to satisfy our curiosity; we seek an answer to calm our cries.

Is the Epicurean dilemma the last word on the subject? Do Christianity's critics state the problem in such a way that we must simply let it rest, unresolved, with no cogent defense of our Creator? Must we concede that perhaps God is not good, or perhaps he's not able, or perhaps he's both but just wasn't wise enough to prevent these things to begin with? Our hearts cannot settle for that. We cannot deny the existence of evil, and we cannot sacrifice the power or the goodness of God. We can't embrace superficial philosophies that say A plus B plus C disproves our faith. We have personal questions that simplistic philosophies don't address. We must keep digging.

2

Love, Power, and
a Whole Lot of Evil

Leper: *"If you will, you can make me clean."*
Jesus: *"I will; be clean."*

Mark 1:40–41

Epileptic's father: *"If you can do anything, have compassion on us and help us."*
Jesus: *"If you can! All things are possible for one who believes."*

Mark 9:22–23

In a sense, it's the Judeo-Christian tradition that poses this Epicurean conundrum to begin with. Those who embrace Judeo-Christian theology believe God is sovereign, all-powerful, infinitely able to address any situation from his unlimited supply of power. He who spoke the universe into being and continues to sustain it has no difficulty intervening in any part of his creation, according to the theology we derive from the Bible. At the same time, we believe God is love—love guides his actions, and his desire for every human being is motivated by goodwill and compassion. But if God is infinitely able to intervene in our suffering, and he is infinitely loving toward us, why doesn't he step in and do something when catastrophe strikes?

We have no trouble understanding why God lets us go through difficulties that help us grow and deepen our relationship with him. We can see the purpose in trials that strengthen us and shape us. What we really wrestle with are the debilitating crises God does not prevent, even when they result in our ultimate harm. We see hardships that seem to produce nothing in the lives of those who experience them. We see that God lets people suffer excruciating pain, often with no apparent redemptive purpose—he even lets them die and go to hell—and we have a hard time reconciling that with the belief that he defines his character as loving.

God Won't?

There are two unbiblical, pseudo-Christian ways of dealing with the dilemma. They seem somewhat compatible with Christianity on the surface, but they are not. One approach is to compromise God's loving character. No one actually phrases it this way, but there are all sorts of concepts of God that make him impersonal or indifferent. Deism, for example—the belief that God set the world in motion but pretty much leaves it to run its course—is one way of doing this. Since God created the world, deist theology says, he is powerfully able to intervene to relieve the suffering of humankind if he wants to, but the fact that he does not indicates that he must not want to. He is like a watchmaker who wound us up and now leaves us alone. Or perhaps he even lovingly watches us "from a distance," as one popular song several years ago proposed. There are variations on this theme, but they all come down to an impersonal creator God—an absentee landlord, so to speak. It is an unbiblical picture, obviously, if we are to retain belief in any of the intervening miracles and guidance God has given his people in Scripture and in the centuries since.

The God of the Bible is the God who opens the waters for his people to pass through, who enables Davids to slay oppressive Goliaths, who reveals his will through the law and the prophets, who even clothed himself in a human body and entered the world in order to save us. He is not lacking in love, not in any book of the Bible—even in the ones full of harsh judgment. He is no absentee God. He is anything but disinterested. Instead, we are given a picture of a God who is always intimately involved in his creation, answering the prayers of his people and involving them in his mission. We can believe in the distant watchmaker God if we want to, but we have to throw out the Bible if we do. The God of the Bible does not lack for loving involvement.

God Can't?

The other unbiblical response, the one more in vogue in our generation, is to compromise God's power. This response has been adopted by many of those who believe in a generic creator God with no personality—a force or original source of some sort—but it has been adopted at some level by many Christian theologians as well. The theory is that God's mastery of creation is limited in some way or another. Again, that God just isn't biblical; the validity of Scripture must be sacrificed to believe in such a deity.

Scripture aside, this idea of a less-than-omnipotent God is disturbing. The thought that the world is somehow out of control, beyond God's ability to sovereignly govern, is alarming, especially in the face of our tragedies. No one in the midst of a crisis finds comfort in a God who wishes he could help but can't. This idea is especially disturbing, and surprising, when it comes from within the church. We don't expect people who derive their spiritual heritage from the Bible to proclaim a God so far removed from it. But that false teaching is among us. After the infamous terrorist attacks on the United States, for example, a pastor preached a sermon on his answer to the question, Where was God on September 11? His answer was that perhaps God was not able to stop the attack.

Not able? What God was he talking about? The God who simultaneously created the mind-boggling expanse of the universe and the intricate complexities of cells and atoms? The God who holds a universe of stars much larger than our sun in the palm of his hand? The God who put into each nucleus enough genetic information to exceed the ability of our most powerful computers to thoroughly process it? A local tribal deity, perhaps, would have been unable to stop the attacks of September 11, but if we say that the God who laid down the physical laws of this universe, who established the very laws by which hijacked airplanes remain airborne and by which fuel combusts, is powerless to intervene in the same laws he created, we have one bizarre concept of God. What sense does it make to believe that the creator of physical laws is captive to them?

Those of us who adhere to biblical authority can also dismiss this explanation. It isn't satisfying at all, especially in our trials. That sort of God does nothing to encourage us when we're in pain. The God of the Bible is not impotent, not by any means. He is repeatedly portrayed as actively sovereign—the heavens were created to declare his glory, and he sustains his entire creation. He counts the hairs on our heads, and he knows when the sparrow falls. He is a very present help in trouble, he calms the winds and the waves, he can protect us in a lion's den or a fiery furnace, he is able to part the waters and deliver his people, and he is master over disease, death, and sin. There are certainly times when he does not deliver his people from evil, but it isn't because he can't. There's no limit to the power of the God of the Bible.

God Doesn't?

A more biblical approach that falls under the category of compromising God's power asserts that God has voluntarily limited himself by the natural laws he has set in place—at least since biblical times. It isn't that he *can't* intervene because he isn't powerful enough or that he *won't* intervene because he is apathetic or distant. This view states, rather, that he chooses not to intervene because he has ordained that his power will operate within the boundaries he himself has set. The physical laws of this universe are inviolable, and he doesn't compromise his creation by supernaturally intervening in our affairs. His love and power would let him, but his rules won't. This is certainly more plausible and consistent with the biblical picture of God, at least on the surface. It's true that God has, in fact, put physical laws into place, and, from our observation, he almost always abides by them. But this view is still not Christian or even remotely true. According to the Bible, God *has* superseded his own natural laws. His sovereignty *has* crossed the boundaries that govern our normal lives. He *has* answered prayers, and not always

31

according to the mechanics of this physical world. He *has* demonstrated his power.

The Bible testifies to numerous supernatural events, and if we say God doesn't overrule the natural, we have to throw out the Bible, including its God, whom we still say we believe in. We would have to eliminate our own belief in all of God's miracles, including the resurrection of Jesus—in which case, we might as well reject Christianity altogether. We would have to ignore water turned into wine, the healing of lepers, the blind given sight, the lame leaping, and all the miraculous answers to prayer we have ever received or heard about. This view is tantamount to suggesting that God gave us a revelation full of wonderful, supernatural events and then told us not to expect anything other than his strict confinement to natural laws. It's as if God said, "Here's your handbook, the history of my dealings with my people. But don't count on the things it tells you. It's just symbolism." Or as if he said, "Here's how I used to deal with people. Isn't that wonderful? But it's all spiritual now. Don't take this literally by any means." Even if one believes God once did miracles and no longer does, the ancient record indicates that there's nothing lacking in his ability or compassion. If God gave us a Bible full of the supernatural and then told us it doesn't apply anymore, that would raise all sorts of other questions about his goodness. That kind of divine bait and switch borders on sadism, compromising not only God's power but also his love. Such a God simply isn't recognizable in the Bible. He doesn't exist there.

The biblical witness is inescapable. God's Word tells us he is sovereign and his power is unlimited. It also tells us he is the embodiment of love. As difficult as it is to reconcile these two assertions that, in tandem, rail against our experience of suffering, it is impossible to dismiss one of them without dismissing the very revelation that tells us of God to begin with. If we compromise God's attributes because our experience doesn't seem to bear them out, we are placing experience above revelation, and once we have done that, we have no business believing anything specific about the Creator at all.

Jesus affirmed the "competing" attributes of God in his ministry as well. To the leper who said, "If You are willing, You can heal me," he said, "I am willing" (Mark 1:40–41 NASB). To the father of a demon-possessed boy, who said, "If You can do anything, take pity on us and help us," Jesus responded with a laugh. "'If You can?' All things are possible to him who believes" (Mark 9:22–23 NASB). An affirmation of both God the Father's and God the Son's love *and* power, with no compromise to either, is explicit in Jesus's teaching. There's absolutely no contradiction in his teaching between God's willingness to intervene and his ability to do so. The psalmist confirms it too: "One thing God has spoken, two things have I heard: that you, O God, are strong, and that you, O Lord, are loving" (Ps. 62:11–12 NIV). There it is, all spelled out for us. The God compromisers who wrestle with the problem of evil have to reject emphatic statements in the Bible to make their points. We're given assurance: yes, he loves us, and, yes, he is all powerful.

Still, we suffer. The wounds of this world continue to fester. Love, power, and evil do coexist. We must look deeper into the biblical revelation to find out why.

Love, Freedom, and Utter Disaster

I remember, as a child, hearing sermons on the problem of evil. Preachers always sought to answer the questions of why God let the serpent into his garden and why he allowed

Adam and Eve to be so gullible. The answers were accurate and perceptive but pretty standard: God wanted a being created in his image who would have the ability to love him. In order for love to be genuine, it has to be freely chosen. In order for it to be freely chosen, the freedom not to choose it has to be available. And given that choice, we blew it. This is the world we ended up with.

This usual evangelical answer to the problem of pain and suffering should be familiar to most believers by now. It's a good, biblical approach, and it's absolutely true. God *could* have created human beings to love him automatically, but that would be a compulsory love born not of choice but of obligation. It wouldn't be genuine. There had to be freedom of choice. And just as the freedom to love God is a necessary part of this capacity for free will, so is the freedom to reject him. The suffering we experience is a result of the freedom that was granted in the name of true love. A world in which bona fide love is a possibility is also a world in which sin and evil are possibilities. We let evil in, and this painful world is the result.

This typical Christian approach to the problem of evil is coherent enough, as far as it goes. It's the primary line of reasoning in C. S. Lewis's *Problem of Pain*—perhaps the most articulate expression of this view but certainly not the only one—and it partially explains why God allowed evil into his creation in the first place. There is nothing unbiblical in the explanation at all. It answers big parts of the question for us.

That's especially true when we turn the question of evil inward—from What's wrong with the world? to What's wrong with me?—for, at some level, we must know that the root of the trouble we see is buried deep within every one of us, not just the moral aberrants of this planet. In Adam's rebellion in the garden, and ours ever since, we have opened up a Pandora's box of pain and evil in this life.

Much of the suffering we experience is the direct result of sin. Violence against fellow human beings has its roots in our sinful, selfish desires, as do theft, slander, divorce, lust, many of our diseases, and any other attitude or behavior that creates dissent and corrupts the flesh. Furthermore, much of our suffering is an indirect result of sin. Natural disasters, the frailties of old age, the death that comes to all of us—these are, according to the Bible, an implied consequence of living in a fallen world, if not the direct product of specific rebellious acts. We hurt because we—the first man and woman and all who would be their descendants—left the sanctuary of the garden by disobeying God and interrupting our relationship with him. We have no one to blame but ourselves. Even when the suffering seems to be the result of an act of God—a tornado, a volcano, a flood—we are told that the world as it was originally created did not include such devastation. We experience it because we rebelled.

The Deeper Question

But there's another question underlying this logical explanation. Why God let Adam and Eve choose evil isn't the question that nags at me. I understand about the necessity of choosing between love and its evil alternative, but that's not entirely satisfying for some reason. There's a deeper question. Why would a God of foresight allow the choice to begin with? What was so compelling about creatures who would love him that it would make this creation business worthwhile? Sure, the payoff would be huge if we in fact did choose to love him. But a God of foresight knew we wouldn't, at least not without considerable trauma first. So what's in this for him?

God's creation of a world in which free will—and, consequently, genuine love—is a possibility often comes across as a calculated risk that didn't pay off. Redemption is often portrayed as a backup plan implemented by God after the fall rather than as God's ordained plan before creation. We know, of course, that shortsightedness is not a biblical attribute of God, and we usually aren't explicit about this nagging question that hangs in the back of our minds about God's advance knowledge of the fall. We know that God does have foresight, that he knew about the fall before it happened, and that he let it happen, all according to his wisdom from before the foundation of the world. We just struggle with the why of it all, because we know if we were faced with such a risk, we would not go through with it. We would not have proceeded with a plan that included such pain. But God did.

This mystery wreaks havoc on otherwise neat theologies. Behind all we say or do as Christians, behind the celebration and joy that come with our new life in Christ, this one unalterable fact remains: people still suffer profoundly, and God still lets them.

Our biblical explanations of love and free will take the blame off God's shoulders and put it on man's, but the fact still remains: God knew about our rebellion and ensuing grief ahead of time, and he still went through with the plan. We experience genuine agony, and, for many, that agony is irreconcilable and eternal, if we are to believe the Bible's assertions about hell. We are a badly damaged creation, and many of us will never recover. Even after we have been reconciled to him, we still may have to experience unspeakable anguish until his kingdom comes in full. We will get sick, we will watch loved ones suffer, our emotions will be tested by what we see, our bodies will waste away, and we will die.

Yes, we sinned. Yes, we deserve it. We have all knowingly committed treason at one time or another against the infinite Creator and source of life. But the sovereign, loving God knew about all this before it ever happened, and he ordained it anyway! There *has* to be some rational explanation. We want to understand why God knowingly did all this for love—or if there was some other motivation involved. Somehow, in the end, the benefits surely must exceed the cost, and we struggle to see how they do. There must be something, some lens through which to see this, that makes it all look right.

3

God Knew

The creation was subjected to futility, not willingly, but because of him who subjected it, in hope that the creation itself will be set free from its bondage to decay and obtain the freedom of the glory of the children of God.

Romans 8:20–21

The question of why evil is in the world is bigger than the usual evangelical answer we've always heard. The traditional Christian answer isn't wrong; it's just incomplete. It answers the question only to a point. It doesn't go far enough; something still disturbs us. Somewhere in the back of our minds, we know: God knew ahead of time about the fall, and he still created us.

We can't blame God for creating an evil world, of course. He is not evil's author, and he did not create anything in a fallen state. We *have* to emphasize that. The philosophical First Cause never subjected anything (or anyone) to corruption when he first "caused" this cosmos. But he did create a world he knew would eventually fall. We can never blame him for anything related to evil, but we can acknowledge that he had prior awareness of it. He affirms his own foreknowledge over and over again in Scripture. Evil didn't just secretly slip in under God's sovereign radar. The plan of salvation was in place before the foundation of the world, we are told. He knew ahead of time we would need saving.

In Genesis, we're given little glimpses of the state of the garden, of what life in a pristine creation was like. We know God walked with the man and the woman in some palpable way. We know his words were clear. We know Adam and Eve lacked nothing and were fully content with what they had been given. We can't imagine that kind of environment, at least not with any sense of realism. We might imagine it as an escapist imagines his own internal fantasies, but we don't really think we can ever return to Eden. All we know is that things were great, and now they're not. And we're given only a skeletal outline as to why.

But let's imagine the scene. What was going on in the Garden of Eden that day? Was this omniscient, omnipresent God who often walked with Adam and Eve somehow absent and unaware? Was the hands-on blesser suddenly distracted from his beautiful creation? And why did he put the forbidden tree "in the midst of the garden," where it was hard to avoid, in the first place (Gen. 2:9 NASB)? Were Eve and the serpent then left completely alone, unmonitored and unnoticed? That seems to be the implication of the Genesis text, but we know from the rest of Scripture that this can't be true. God is omnipresent, for one thing, and he also had a very tangible relationship with Adam and Eve (Gen. 3:8). God's voice was clearly audible when he commanded which trees were good and which one wasn't. A creation he looked upon and blessed as inherently good—he said so himself after each day of creation—could not have lamented a distant God. No, the omniscient God who regularly walked with the first couple was not unaware that day. He certainly knew of the serpent. And he just watched.

The common explanation given for his passivity, as we've observed, is that to have done otherwise would have abrogated our freedom, and without freedom, our love means nothing, because it isn't really chosen love. But isn't there some middle ground between silence and control? Don't we usually take this middle ground with our own children? We recognize their free will, and we can't force them to love us, but we plead with them and give them ample reasons to follow our directions and trust our love. We have ways of reminding them of our will without forcing them to follow it. We'll whisper in their ears or even shout to their faces in order to keep them from making a mess of their lives, knowing all the while that the ultimate choice is theirs. God, the loving Father, could have whispered and reminded like all loving parents do when their children are about to devastate their own lives, and it wouldn't have denied humanity's free will.

We have no evidence of that kind of thing going on in Genesis. As far as we know, God didn't step in and explain to Eve—even while respecting her free will—about all the dreadful consequences of eating from that tree. Would even just a little reminder have diverted her love from her self-interested self and pointed it toward the trustworthy God?

Perhaps a perfect love and trust of God should have been enough, and any further pleading would have only diminished it and resulted in a more subtle sin of self-will. Perhaps a God who reminded would have been only nagging his children into submission rather than patiently waiting for their love.

But couldn't he have said *something*? Apparently not. There is absolutely nothing—no diversion, no explanation, not even a whisper from God to counter the wiles of the serpent who seemed to be so carelessly butchering God's words. There is no voice from above saying, "Eve, don't believe him; that's not exactly what I said. The choice is entirely yours, of course, but just know that he isn't telling you the truth." One little word like that could have maintained Eve's free will while preventing all the heartache, all the pain, all the death and destruction this world has known in the generations since. There's no word to Adam either. God could have said, "Adam, the choice is entirely yours, of course, but I want you to know that you're about to give up nearly all the blessings I've given you. You're on the brink, faced with a choice between your wife and me. Go ahead and choose, but that's what's at stake." But no. He just watched.

Why? That annoying question won't go away, even with an apologetic of the free will of man and how free will is necessary for genuine love.

It gnaws at us, doesn't it? Deep down, no matter how much we explain human freedom and the reason for our race of love-capable beings, we know God knew ahead of time what was at stake and he still let it all happen. He let humanity come to the end of its innocence without so much as a whisper of intervention. He who is not surprised by anything—who has ordained all our days ahead of time (Ps. 139:15–16)—was silent on that particular day. It was already written in his records. So were all the days of suffering and excruciating pain the world has ever known since then. On that critical day, the serpent waxed eloquent, but God was quiet. He had powerfully spoken the world into creation, but on its fatal day of rebellion, he became silent. The only voices heard were a crafty voice of deception and the voices of two easily exploited victims-turned-rebels. Before Eve listened to that snake, before Adam mindlessly followed along, God knew. He knew everything. And he still let it happen.

God's Not to Blame

Don't misunderstand: we should never blame God for evil. Suffering is in this world because we willingly invited it in. We have taken huge bites of forbidden fruit, and we have often taken them with gusto. If we want to assign blame for evil, we should look to the unholy coalition between the archenemy of God and the corruptible flesh of humanity, not to God himself. It's a matter of the free will we were given in the garden.

Somehow, though, God's sovereignty is woven into our free will, or our free will is woven into his sovereignty—whichever way you want to look at it. The relationship between our free will and his sovereignty is indeed mysterious, and it is so intricate that Joseph is able to say of his brothers' horrific act of selling him into slavery, "You meant evil against me, but God meant it for good" (Gen. 50:20). (We want to say that God *allowed* it for good, but the text says he *meant* it—with some level of intention.) Sovereignty and free will are intertwined when the Bible says of Pharaoh's sinful choices that God had hardened his heart. And, for an example of suffering not specifically tied to evil acts, a blind man's painful situation in John 9 existed in order that—so that, for the specific purpose that—God's glory might be demonstrated (v. 3). Sovereignty and suffering are mysteriously, but inextricably and unarguably (from a biblical point of view), woven together.

Now, if Joseph can say his brothers meant their treachery for evil (free will) but God meant it for good (sovereignty), we can also say of the introduction of evil into this world that Adam, Eve, and Satan meant it for rebellion (free will), but God meant it for his glory (sovereignty). And that latter aspect is what this book is about. We will never precisely understand the relationship between God's sovereignty and our evil, but we have to accept that it is consistent with the mysterious God of the Bible. We don't know exactly why God was silent on the day the serpent spoke, but we have to accept that he was not blindsided by this turn of events. For some mysterious reason, it was ordained.

We continue to ask our why question, because that's astounding to us. Is love so valuable that it's worth millions living excruciating lives of anxiety, dread, hunger, and conflict? Is it so valuable that it's worth the eternal torment of billions of unbelievers? We know that if we were the creator of the garden, we would have tended it with a greater zeal for protecting its purity—especially if we were eternal and entirely self-sufficient. What would an utterly content creator have to gain from such a gambit? Why would he accept those stakes? We might have wanted love but not at such an ugly cost. The pain of the fallen soul is something we try to flee from our whole lives. We would not have said, "It's better to have loved and lost than never to have loved at all." The cost of this kind of love is too high for us.

But it's not too high for God, apparently. The fall of humanity didn't creep up on an unaware deity. Just as Eve and then Adam made a choice, God had made a prior choice. He knew all about the deal that was going to go down in the garden. He allowed it of his own will, and he did it for love. And, as we shall see, he did it for glory.

Bad Things, Good People

For many people, no motivation of God for allowing evil is plausible. Some years ago Harold Kushner wrote a book titled *When Bad Things Happen to Good People.* The rabbi related his struggles with the problem of pain, prompted largely by his son's struggle with a disease that led to his early death. It was a touching, heartfelt meditation on this intractable problem that has perplexed thinking people of all generations. Many have read Rabbi Kushner's book and found comfort there—not answers, perhaps, but certainly companionship. It was even required reading in one of my seminary classes, primarily because it shed light on counseling people in grief but also because it was an attempt to address this question that has been nagging at us. Here was a religious leader who was honest enough to say, "I don't have all the answers, but I have found meaning in the suffering." It drew a sympathetic reading from many fellow sufferers.

I certainly mean no offense to the rabbi, and I grieve with him over the loss of his son. That was one of the many tragic consequences of this broken world and further evidence that something has gone horribly wrong. Deaths like that are one of the reasons we keep asking this question, and at least the rabbi was honest with his feelings about it. But I did not find any comfort in his book.

One of his premises is that the cosmos is still being put in order by the one who created it. It's a process, and we're living in an age when the process is yet incomplete. The Hebrew text in Genesis implies that the world began with chaos: It was "formless and void" when the Creator said, "Let there be light" (Gen. 1:1–2 NASB). But Kushner suggests that creation wasn't entirely ordered after seven days, or even seven eons, as many interpreters of Genesis argue. Kushner proposes, rather, that God is still bringing order out of that chaos and that much of our lives is still in the yet untouched part of it.

It doesn't bring me any comfort simply to think that one day, ages and eons hence, God will complete his work and all this disorder will be eliminated—unredeemed and unprofitable now but done away with then. Those of us who live in the chaos want some sense of meaning now, or at least soon—something more than just being a part of a zillion-year evolution in God's own struggle with evil. We want to know that the evil in our lives is redeemable and not just an unfortunate learning experience for the God who made us. We want to know that someday soon it will make sense.

Not only is Kushner's premise lacking in comfort, but it is also intellectually unsatisfying. It isn't consistent with Scripture, and it doesn't really fit with historical, mainstream Judaism or Christianity, despite the fact that some theologians from both traditions have incorporated it into their thinking. Deep down, we know that evil is not just an unwarranted intrusion on otherwise good and innocent people. We've had a part in bringing it here.

Who Is Good?

When I was teaching a class in international politics at a local university, one of my students wanted to talk to me about her grade. It was a little confusing trying to get to the basis of her complaint. She agreed that she had missed the questions I had marked. She knew she hadn't mastered the material. After some discussion, I found out what the real problem was: she felt that since she was paying a lot for her education, I was, in effect, her employee. In her mind, she felt entitled to a diploma and an impressive transcript. She and I were operating under two different mental contracts. I thought I was assessing how well she had learned the material; she thought she was buying credentials.

We do that with God. We bring one contract into our relationship with him, while he has specified another. Our assumed mental contract is that if we are faithful to him and live a reasonably righteous life, he should make everything, or at least the really major things, work out for us. We think we should get his favor because we've lived up to the contract—*our* contract. And we always define his favor in our own terms.

With that in mind, let's examine Kushner's premise about bad things and good people. We have no argument over what constitutes a bad thing, but we get into some shaky theology when we talk about good people. Sure, the Bible affirms that there are obedient and disobedient, righteous and unrighteous. But it doesn't let us get away with calling ourselves inherently good. Psalm 14:1–3 emphatically assures us that "there is no one who does good" (NIV), and Paul elaborates on that assertion—more than that, he powerfully hammers it into his readers—in Romans 3. All have sinned, no one is righteous, and we fall far, far short of the glory of God. We were inherently good as God made us, but everyone born since that fateful day in the lost garden has been born defective.

If that's offensive, take a moment to consider the evidence. We know we have all broken a multitude of God's commandments, but why quibble about minor dos and don'ts when we can go straight to the biggest failure of all? Who among us can claim to have kept the single most important commandment, even for a single hour? "You shall love the LORD your God with all your heart and with all your soul and with all your might" (Deut. 6:4). Have you done that? I haven't. Our God asks for our complete love, yet we give it so sporadically, so faintly, so apathetically that it can hardly be called love at all.

This is the first and foremost of the commandments, a monumental, landmark imperative, the ultimate law and the foundation for all other divine laws—so designated by Jesus and a good number of rabbis—and yet we can't keep it. Surely, our failure to do so must be considered the greatest sin of all. Maybe we have moments when we're obedient to this word, but a few moments of obedience cannot make us good. No, we know we've had a part in inviting evil to this planet and welcoming it with open arms. We haven't even passed the basic test of loving our Creator. We can't just blame our sin on God or Satan. "We all, like sheep, have gone astray" (Isa. 53:6 NIV). So why, to ask Kushner's question, do bad things happen to good people? First find a truly good person—an unfallen, perfectly compliant soul—and then maybe we can take that question seriously.

But there's more to this approach that makes it unpalatable. I cannot believe in a God who, on the one hand, parts the sea in order to deliver his people from the hand of a relentless pharaoh yet, on the other hand, is partly bound by the evil that plagues us all. Either God is sovereign or he is not. The God of our Bible is—over and over again. We are not given much evidence in the Bible of a deity whose world is beyond his own control. It's contradictory for Kushner or any biblical teacher to find in the God of the Bible Israel's national identity and its ultimate experience of deliverance and then to turn around and say this God is not able to deliver. No, God is not impotent if the biblical witness is at all true. The Bible may not give us a clear answer about why evil is in the world, but it is clear about the power and majesty of the sovereign, almighty God. There is no way we can refer to him as the Ancient of Days, the Alpha and Omega, the everlasting Father, and the King of Kings and still propose that he might be reluctantly struggling with evil—and losing sometimes.

In fact, the one book Kushner uses to support his thesis about God's struggle is Job, the same book in which the Almighty points out the tenuous position of those who question his power. God laid the foundation, he was there at the beginning, and he put all things in motion. Not only does he not struggle with Leviathan, he doesn't even have to allow Leviathan to exist. The beast is no threat. Evil has not gotten out of hand in spite of God's best efforts; it has gotten out of hand for a reason. There simply must be a reason if we are to maintain any belief in an omnipotent God.

Beyond the Triangle

But that's part of the predicament, isn't it? The traditional way of stating the problem is that one of the three points of the triangle must be invalid. We cannot maintain the existence of evil, the love of God, and the omnipotence of God all at the same time, so we are told. Yet we know that evil exists; we see its carnage daily. We certainly don't want to compromise the love of God unless we want to do away with him altogether. Who wants to believe in a dispassionate or even malevolent deity? So it only stands to reason that Kushner and others would propose that God isn't all that omnipotent. His omnipotence is the only thing left in the triangle. And yet, for those of us who hold to the integrity of a God who has revealed himself in the words of Scripture, we cannot compromise that point. There must be another factor to consider. There must be some way around this conundrum. There must be some key to the puzzle that makes it make sense.

There is. Most theologians, for obvious reasons, have suggested that the missing piece of the puzzle will remain missing for the rest of our earthly existence. It is sealed up in the mind of God, and he will, by necessity, hold his higher ways secret to our finite minds. That's a plausible way to approach the problem, and, to an extent, it's true. After all, it only makes sense that there are going to be some things about an infinite creator that small, finite brains simply are not going to be able to comprehend. It is certainly reasonable to say that the three-point problem is too simply posited. Eternal realities are rarely reducible to such a bare frame. We can assume a greater complexity, one that we will never fully understand. Most of evangelical Christianity is content to assert that all three points are true: evil exists, yet God is both loving and powerful. There is an answer, we believe, but we cannot find it. We settle into a trust that perhaps one day, a day in the eternal kingdom, it will be clear.

Perhaps so. But perhaps there are some clues in this revelation from God that we have missed—or seen many times before but dismissed as insufficient. I'd like to revisit some of those clues. I think there are some hints in Scripture that can take us deeper into the problem than we've usually gone. No, I'm not suggesting that the problem is hereby solved or that the biblical answers are complete and clearly laid out. Obviously, they aren't, or the multitude of great thinkers who have probed these depths would have discovered them. But I do believe there are answers better than our religious philosophers have given us, better than the other great faiths of the world have given us, and better than even many evangelicals have given us. Most of us haven't gone deep enough.

Our God insists on depth. Life demands that we probe this question, and we can't be content to let depressing headlines speak for themselves while the church remains silent. We have things to say about this problem, things that will help a hurting world. We must figure out what to say.

4

Long Ago in Heaven

Let us make man in our image, after our likeness.

Genesis 1:26

Imagine being allowed to hear a conversation within the Holy Trinity before the foundation of the world. Granted, it's a huge stretch of the imagination for us fallen mortals, but try anyway. Suppose you are a privileged angel in the throne room of God, and you hear the counsel within the Godhead of how to make himself known in all of his attributes. Suppose no Lucifer-led rebellion has yet occurred. All heaven is in order. Obedient angels sing God's praises. All is light, and there is no darkness at all. No conflict. No violence. No bitterness. Just peace and joy in the presence of God. Here God can demonstrate his holiness, his love, the radiance of his glory, his wisdom, his kindness, and a host of other attributes. After all, it is his inclination to share himself. He has created all things in order to be known and loved for who he is, and there is an appreciative audience in this heaven that honors his perfect character and rejoices in it. As far as it can.

But there are aspects of his character that *cannot* be known in this heavenly context. There is no framework for understanding some of his most precious attributes, no canvas on which he can spread out his most beautiful colors. From your imaginary privileged position, would you hear the angels singing praises for God's mercy? If so, on what basis? To whom was he merciful before sin? Would you hear of his ability to deliver, heal, and defend? How? Whom did he deliver, heal, or defend before the fall?

In your innocent eavesdropping on the conversation within the Trinity, some of these concepts may sound strange to your ears—mercy, forgiveness, deliverance, healing. You know of God's intense desire to be known, but you have no frame of reference for understanding any of these things. They're hidden attributes in this perfect milieu. If you continued listening to the Triune conversation, you might hear how the staging of another context might occur. And, in the process, you would understand how the perfections of heaven are an unsuitable reference point for many of the most glorious attributes of our God. How, for example, can a merciful God show mercy in a world that has not erred? How can he show himself as Warrior or Conqueror without enemies? How can he show himself as Deliverer unless there is a captivity? Or Refuge unless there is a threat? Or Healer unless there is a sickness? Or Forgiver unless wrongs have been committed? He can't. There are no logical options for displaying these characteristics without there first being objects of mercy, deliverance, healing, and so on. And for these objects to be present, the imperfect has to come.

Or what if, at the time of your heavenly privilege of over-hearing sacred plans, there had already been an angelic re-bellion? Perhaps Lucifer had already attempted his coup and was under the impending judgment of God. We can envision him, according to his accusing nature, leveling blasphemous charges against the Creator he once worshiped. "You're un-merciful," he might say if he'd ever contemplated the con-cept of mercy. "You're incapable of redeeming your own creation. You're not as loving as you suggest. You aren't in control after all, are you? We can go to depths where you cannot follow."

This is not a far-fetched conversation if we are to believe Job 1. In that text the adversary charges that God's good attributes are effective only when all is well in his creation. The clear accusation is that God's goodness is not enough to sustain a creature in turmoil, that somehow his love extends only so far and no farther, that all of his good attributes are deficient somehow, or severely limited. They don't apply in worst-case scenarios. Perhaps this creation we're a part of is a contradiction of the adversary's slanderous charge. Perhaps God said, "There's a side of me you just don't understand. My mercy can extend to the very depths of depravity. You haven't seen anything yet." And, behold, our world was spoken into existence.

The Rational God

This is all speculation, of course. We aren't granted the privilege of being insiders to divine counsel. God answers Job with statements of his supreme right to conduct his creation however he wills, with implicit trust being our only appropriate response. He does not explain himself to Job, and he does not explain himself to us. We can never know the complexities of his ways, which, as we are told, are far above our understanding. What we can know is this: our God is intensely rational. He does not create worlds in which the costs outweigh the benefits. However much we suffer, however costly this existence seems to be, if we are to believe in the biblical God, we must believe that there is a reason for suffering. Pain has a purpose.

That is why the above conversation before the foundation of the world, as speculative as it is, seems to make sense. If the purpose of creation as we know it is to display attributes of God that cannot be displayed in a perfect world, then this creation, with all its evil and suffering, is entirely logical. To say otherwise is to say we were created by an irrational God. That's an assertion gladly considered by the skeptic trying to puncture an evangelical belief system, but it's not biblical. No, the existence of this fallen world is extremely rational *given its purpose*. If God desires to make himself known, to be loved fully by his creatures of free will, and some of his most marvelous, praiseworthy characteristics are revealed only in the context of their antithesis, then this is exactly the kind of world one would expect to find as the backdrop for his revelation. It is an appropriate stage for the Main Character to show his range.

Is this logical? Absolutely. In fact, it's a pretty basic premise. There can be no mercy in a perfect world, by the very definition of what we call mercy. The omnipotent God simply cannot show mercy unless someone needs it. That attribute is completely obscured until some foil, some object, reflects it. That's our role in creation; we're the ones who need it and who reflect it. We may not enjoy that calling, but it's ours from the moment of the fall. Our God is rational in all he does, and if he chooses to be known in his mercy, it absolutely must be in an imperfect world. There have to be objects of mercy. There is no other way.

Is this a biblical premise? Unquestionably. Story after story in the Bible shows God revealing his hidden attributes in the context of pain and suffering. God created. Evil entered in through moral free agency. And God began his redemptive plan. Jesus told his disciples, "Nothing is hidden except to be made manifest; nor is anything secret except to come to light" (Mark 4:22). If that principle applies to the gospel, as it does in this verse, might it also apply to some core attributes of a merciful God? Might it apply to the author of the gospel as well as to the gospel itself? God's redemptive plan, we are told, has its foundations in eternity past. We can assume he played it out on this planet for a reason. He created us for one obvious reason: to make himself known.

Revelation Hurts

That's the premise in the pages that follow. Somewhere in eternity past, before evil was ever allowed to exist, God was known only in those characteristics that could be demonstrated in an untainted environment. His glory, while unlimited in its essence, was limited in its expression. The core of his being was essentially unknown. So there came into existence, by the wisdom of the Godhead from before the foundation of the world, a necessary background designed to further accentuate these visible characteristics and to reveal his hidden attributes to a watching universe. Evil and its hideous consequence, suffering, were allowed to show up. It wasn't pleasant, not for evil's hosts, like us, and certainly not for the God who hates evil. But it had to be so. Mercy cannot come without a needy recipient, so God designed a race that would become incredibly needy by its own self-destructive hand. The result is a creation that groans for its redemption.

We think our groaning is a product of unknowable mysteries, and from our perspective it often is. But, in reality, our condition is purposeful; this creation that groans for its redemption exists to display the marvels of a Redeemer. To us, evil and suffering seem to be intractable, permanent aspects of existence. But they are not permanent at all. They are a temporary condition that will forever witness to the attributes of God that were once concealed in heavenly places. For all eternity, every created being will be able to look back at what once was a suffering planet and say, "Oh, *that's* what grace is! *That's* what redemption looks like. *That's* what it means to be healed." Or, better yet, they will focus on the Person: "So *that's* what our God is really like! We had no idea."

And for many of us—those of us who have human free will and a capacity to know both the pleasure and the pain of love—it will be more than observation; it will be experiential knowledge. Before there was evil, God's manifold mercies could not have been known or even seen. Now they can be. And that's what is ultimately important.

The Rescuer God

> Call upon me in the day of trouble; I will deliver you, and you shall glorify me.
>
> Psalm 50:15

There's a reason that fairy tales with happy endings resonate with the depths of our souls—we are part of one. That's why every culture on the planet has such stories and why all boys and girls envision them for their lives. Deep down inside, we know life is supposed to turn out right. Things are supposed to be resolved. The wounds cannot remain open forever.

Our fairy tale, unlike the bedtime stories, is very real and very true. It is the fountainhead of all the fictional tales. Its story line has many imitators. There's a maiden in distress—that's us—and an evil, traitorous enemy of the throne—and we all know who that is. Then there's a rescuing Prince. We who understand the New Testament know who that is too. This fairy tale is a drama that runs deep in the human psyche, because the human psyche was created for the drama God planned to unfold. As authors like John Eldredge and Brent Curtis, among others, have so profoundly explained, there is a sacred romance being played out on the stage of the human experience.

This romance displays God in all his glory, from righteous judgment to tender mercy and from utter wholesome purity to a deep divine jealousy. We see the good Prince's commitment to and passion for his beloved. We see his skill and cunning in defeating the enemy. We see his bravery and devotion in his relentless pursuit to make things right. We ooh and aah over the beauty and purity of his love. In this broken world, on this dark stage, we get to see the range of God's character. We get to see the drama of rescue and redemption, the passion of purity and romance, the heart of the beloved and the daring of the Prince's quest. It's the greatest play the universe has ever known.

But it's more than a romantic play to us. That's because we're in the middle of it, after the conflict has been introduced but before it has been resolved. We're between act 1 and the final bows, and things are pretty tense. We can read a fairy tale with little suspense, because we know how it's going to end. But the children to whom we read aren't sure. For them, everything is at stake before the rescuing prince arrives. They feel the anxiety and anguish of the needy, captive maiden. They identify with her despair.

In the telling of the story of this planet, we're more like the listening children than like the parents reading the story. We have the text, of course, and we know how it ends—just like our children who have heard the story before. But it's still somewhat new to us, and we're not quite sure it's going to end according to the script. We feel the despair because we are the captive maiden. We crave rescue, groan for redemption, and yearn for fulfillment. Mainly, we just want the Prince to show up. We think he'll come for us. He said he would, and he seems trustworthy. But the final act has not been played in our lives, and we're still held captive in a fallen world. We feel the pain.

We know how to read a fairy tale to the kids without much suspense, but we don't know how to live one without it. That's part of the faith process; as we grow in faith, we come to count on the ending with more certainty. We don't let the suspense paralyze us anymore, because we are learning to embrace the final act as it has been taught to us. We believe the resolution will be fantastic, because the Prince—who, as we suspected, is unquestionably trustworthy—has promised that it will be. Meanwhile, when faith is weak or threatened and the suspense creeps back in, we hurt and feel alone.

As hopeless and devastated as we feel sometimes, there's design in our condition. We were made with the capacity to fall—and to fall hard. There's a rescuer God whose character is integral to the story. As a fairy tale about a prince who simply fell in love with a maiden would tell us nothing admirable about the prince—falling in love happens all the time with little fanfare—a whole and unbroken creation would tell us nothing of the rescuer God. There would be no story in which he could display his swordplay and his bravery. There would be no adventure or victory. There would be no sweet kiss of gratitude and devotion from his rescued maiden, no relieved heart over the enormity of the rescue. There would be no revelation of who he really is.

Molded for God

In ancient times, marvelously detailed statues were made to represent the deities of the local culture. In many places in the world, they still are. We have examples from the civilizations of antiquity—Egypt, India, and Greece, among others—as well as numerous modern examples in many Hindu and Buddhist temples around the world.

Have you ever thought about how these statues are made? First some sort of mold—a negative image, actually—is shaped from clay or another hard material. That's a somewhat violent process, as the clay is pushed and poked and forced into the proper shape as a reverse receptacle for its higher purpose. Then molten bronze is poured into the mold. It fills every crevice, perfectly reproducing the details of even delicately modeled shapes. Then after the bronze has hardened, the mold is broken; it is no longer useful. But the beauty of the bronze statue remains, profoundly shaped by the earthen vessel it was poured into and which is no longer needed.

In a way, the real God has cast himself into an earthen mold as well. He is no idol made by human hands, and there's nothing of him to be manufactured—he has always existed in perfect form—but there is something of him to be made visible. He originally made us in his image to reflect his glory, but he foresaw that we would make of this world a negative image that, even in the context of its sin, can still reflect his glory. Our fallen race on this broken planet is full of gaps and valleys and indentations, just like a mold of clay, and it was a violent, self-inflicted process that put us in this shape. But now that we are the proper negative image, the character of the true God can be poured into our broken-ness, filling each corner and scar with delicate precision. In the end, the mold will be broken; the earth *is* passing away, after all, as Scripture declares. But the visibility of the living God will remain because of the casting process to which he subjected himself. This is, in a sense, what the incarnation was about. God cast himself into human flesh—*suffering* human flesh—to be seen and experienced. From the once hollow mold of pain and suffering and evil appears a God of remark-able mercy and comfort and holiness. Those attributes have always been there, but they were not seen. This planet has enhanced God's image—not his essence, but his visibility—in the eyes of all creation. And the image is magnificent.

Pastor Tony Evans gives a comparable illustration in his talks on spiritual warfare. The skill of Michael Jordan, the most celebrated basketball player of our time, came out only in competition. Michael could do the slam dunks, the long jumps, and the twisting, turning shots during warm-ups and practices—but so can a lot of other people. With a qualified opponent on the floor, however, the glory of Michael Jordan's basketball prowess was an amazing thing to behold. It was unique and impossible to fully imitate, though many have modeled themselves after him. The simple fact of the com-petition, the existence of an adversary determined to defeat his team, showed us how Michael could really play. The more intense the competition, the more impressive the display.

So it is with God and this world. The farther we fall, the more impressive his deliverance. The deeper we hurt, the sweeter the comfort. The lonelier we are, the more tender his fellowship. The more we need him, the more we will see him. We never want to (and never should) seek deeper need in order to magnify his goodness; need is just part of who we are. And his merciful character fits into our need like a hand fits into the emptiness of a glove. There is a purpose in the adversity we experience.

If we are to believe in a relentlessly pursuing God—one who is passionate and zealous about revealing himself—then we have to believe that the context in which he pursues us is purposeful. The fall in the Garden of Eden was a tragedy, but it was not an unexpected one. God was not surprised; it was destined. We know that, because we are told much later on—in Ephesians 1, for example—that our redemption was designed before the foundation of the world. God created us with a rescue plan long before we needed rescuing. The last chapter of the story was already written.

All of creation is meant to be a demonstration of God and his handiwork. There are many passages of Scripture that point to that ultimate purpose. But the demonstration of some of God's attributes, the merciful ones, require that at least part of his creation be utterly devastated. Lucky us. That's the role we play. The rescuer God wants a maiden to rescue, and we are that maiden. His swordplay and his bravery—not to mention his zealous passion for his beloved—could not be adequately demonstrated any other way.

When the Pain Is Personal

Let's boil this line of reasoning down to two simple facts and a conclusion.

Simple fact number 1—Everything that was made exists for the glory of God. Numerous Scripture references point to this (Ps. 19:1–3; Rom. 11:36; Col. 1:16, among many more); the Westminster Shorter Catechism points to this ("The chief end of man is to glorify God and enjoy him forever"); the weight of systematic theology throughout the course of church history points to this (Augustine, Aquinas,

Luther, Calvin, etc.). No serious Christian theologian would argue against the idea that human beings specifically, and creation generally, exist for God's glory.

Simple fact number 2—The sovereign God of all knowledge and foresight created a world that would fall and turn tragically evil. Clearly there are those who would argue with God's foresight, but they are vastly outnumbered by those of us who consider his prior knowledge of all history to be foundational and scriptural. As for the existence of evil . . . well, read today's headlines.

Conclusion—There must be something in the context of evil that can glorify God. That is the point of this book, and it applies not only theoretically and theologically but also in your personal daily life.

What does this mean for someone who has just gone through a divorce or someone who has just watched a child die? It means that somewhere in the depth of your grief, there is a God who ministers to you. Hidden attributes of that God are being revealed. You may not see them yet, but you will—that's the whole point. You're a mold being shaped and kneaded into the proper form, and the true deity pours himself into you and your situation every step of the way, both in the pain and in the resolution. If the merciful traits of our God are not seen now and will never be seen, then pain has no purpose, and the Bible's promises are pointless. But pain does have a purpose—multiple purposes, in fact—and the Bible's promises are true. God intervenes. He speaks. And he shows up.

Please do not misunderstand the purpose of this book. It is not just to prove a point; it's to encourage those who suffer by pointing out that there is meaning in their suffering, both in the immediate demonstration of God and in the future glory God shares with his people. That doesn't mean your grief or your hardship isn't real, intense, and excruciating. It does mean, however, that it's real, intense, and excruciating because there's a point to it. We can suffer a lot more if we think it's for a valid reason, so I'm encouraging you to think that way. You aren't in pain pointlessly, not if you trust God in it. My hope in writing is that in the midst of your pain, you will be able to ask God what he is doing in it and you will be patient enough to hear or see him answer. The fact of the matter is that God exists, he knew about evil ahead of time, he ordained our lives, and he stands ready to show himself in one way or another in the context of our grief.

Look for that. If you are going through a personal trial now, there's a purpose in it, and the reason is more than just to develop you into a hardier person. It's true that God uses it to conform you to the image and character of Christ, and any trial is worth the pain for that process alone. But he aims also to *show* you the character of Christ in your trial. Perhaps the revelation is only comfort for now and healing later. Perhaps it's healing and comfort now, with a visible display of God's miraculous power. Perhaps it's something you will only be able to see looking back on it one day from an eternal perspective. His specific plan for your trial may differ from his specific plan for someone else's trial, but there's an aspect of himself to be revealed in it. Trust him. That aspect is there. It's *always* there.

PART 2

THE **PROMISE**

The sufferings of this present time are not worth comparing with the glory that is to be revealed to us.

Romans 8:18

5

The Running God

While he was still a long way off, his father saw him and felt compassion, and ran and embraced him and kissed him.

Luke 15:20

The story of the prodigal son in Luke 15 is one of the most beautiful and memorable parables in the Bible. It paints a picture of God's mercy that an elaborate theology could never provide. The offense of the wayward son in asking for his father's inheritance before his death is so extreme, we're told, that it would have shocked and appalled Jesus's listeners. The depths to which this son fell were so expected and deserved that we are almost surprised at his nerve in returning to his father's household, even with the humility in which he intends to return—as a servant. And the climax of the story, the spectacle of the unabashed father running toward his semirepentant son, is so magnificent, so demonstrative of fatherly love and mercy, that we instinctively crave such a reception from our heavenly Father. It's what our hearts have longed for, and we're delighted that Jesus affirms it as appropriate and welcome.

The parable has several purposes, some of which were quite pointed and offensive to the ruling religious parties of Jesus's time. But the highlight of the story, its defining image, has to be the father's inelegant, undignified sprint toward the returning son.

This son has embarrassed his father with his gall, he has squandered much of what the father worked long and hard to earn, and he stinks. He stinks like those detestable, unclean pigs. Pigs, of course, were prohibited and disdained by Jewish law and were thought of as unworthy scavengers, objects of scorn, pictures of corruption. But this son has already flouted the law and all social protocol. The pigs are simply an apt representation and consequence of his fall, and he now has had his hands all over them. His clothes reek of them. He has craved the pods they ate. Perhaps he has even indulged. There is no clearer picture of destitution than this son, and, as a result, there is no clearer picture of mercy than this father. These few lines of storytelling capture the truth of the gospel better than many full volumes of theology. This is what it's all about.

Have you ever thought about the context that sets up the father's sprint? Have you ever thought about what makes that moment so beautiful, what it reveals about the father's heart, and why the revelation is so dramatic? The answer is so simple that it's hardly worth explanation. Perhaps it's too basic. It's a no-brainer.

What makes this moment of this gospel-defining parable so poignant and so encouraging is the utter depravity of the son. We learn something about the father because the son is not just a little lost but hopelessly lost. He has sunk as low as he can go, fraternizing with prostitutes and swine. He has suffered physical hunger, painful indignity, and perhaps unspeakable guilt—if it ever sinks in just how frivolously he has squandered the father's wealth. His father's welcome is enormously undeserved—and that's precisely why it's such a beautiful picture. Such acceptance is so impressive because the son's departure from righteousness and freedom is so drastic. He has lost all he can possibly lose and offended all he can possibly offend, and it's still not enough to make the father reject him. He's still a son. What incredible mercy! What amazing grace!

Did you catch that? The depravity and the suffering of the son throw into stark relief the character of the father. We would not know who this father is or what he is like if we did not know the excesses of the son. There would be no parable, no point, no story line. Nothing would be learned, no revelation of a father's love, no demonstration of grace that is greater than all our sin. The astounding beauty of this father's love would remain hidden—present but entirely concealed—if no errant son had brought it out of him.

That's the point. The product of the son's sin is a greater knowledge of the father. Depravity leads to revelation. Sin highlights glory. The suffering of humankind sets the stage for the Father's relentless pursuit of his children. We know things about God that we would never have known if we had remained without sin and without pain.

But it's more than just us—*all creation* knows more about God than it would have known had humanity not fallen. Even the cherubim and seraphim who surround him with praises day and night had never seen the Father run. They had never known the depth of his mercy—perhaps they had never known his mercy at all. No son had ever fallen. This whole side of God's character had remained hidden until a redeemable creature appeared.

This is almost too simple to consider, but we should fully expect that if God allowed evil for a reason, the reason is embedded somewhere in Scripture. The story of the prodigal son is one place where the character of the Father is highlighted specifically by the depravity of the son.

A Deeper Tragedy Than Suffering?

Mercy requires an object. It can't be an object that is perfect, because if it were perfect, there would be no need for mercy. No, it requires an object that is fallen, depraved, suffering, and in pain. The mercy of God simply cannot be seen without that. This amazing side of God, this dimension of his personality, could have remained hidden, of course, but that would have been a tragedy of a different sort, much worse in the eternal scheme of things. We lament the condition of our world as a horribly tragic condition, and it is. But have we ever considered that the absence of evil would also have lamentable consequences? So many aspects of the character of God—the ones we praise him most highly for, in fact—are aspects that are invisible without a foil. The question was not whether the tragedy of evil could be avoided. The question was which tragedy to avoid—the tragedy of pain or the tragedy of the substantially hidden God. God chose to accept the former. There's a high cost to revelation. If he is to be revealed in his mercy, there must be evil. The backdrop of imperfection had to be raised.

That's why suffering in this world means something. It sets up a very real stage on which God is demonstrated. As we have discussed, it is not logically possible to have an unfallen world *and* a thoroughly revealed God. So the sacred drama has some awfully ugly elements. It must.

But the *promise* of our pain is just as surely embedded in Scripture as the reason for it is. This promise is clearly demonstrated in the parable of the prodigal son: we who return to the Father in humility and repentance will be welcomed and thrown a party that will more than make up for our generally self-inflicted suffering. Something in the whole rebellion-and-return process will enhance our relationship with the Father. We will see him in ways we've never seen him before, and so will others—the servants, the big brothers, and the readers of the story in the distant future. The parable of the prodigal son is backed by the truth of the redemption story and its God-honoring themes. It gives us a glimpse into the whole plan. It shows us the God who runs with open arms.

Blind for Glory

> His disciples asked him, "Rabbi, who sinned, this man or his parents, that he was born blind?" Jesus answered, "It was . . . that the works of God might be displayed in him."
>
> John 9:2–3

Another hint as to why suffering exists is found in the intriguing interaction between Jesus and his disciples in John 9. There we get a glimpse into the problem of evil from the mouth of God incarnate himself. It's a surprising story, even to those of us who don't hold the same worldview as the disciples. Jesus and the Twelve are passing by a blind man, and it seems an opportune time to ask the Master his opinion on this man's suffering. "Who sinned, this man or his parents?" they ask. Their underlying assumption is revealed: Pain is the result of sin. This man is blind because somebody somewhere did something wrong.

If ever the concept of karma was considered an exclusively Far Eastern phenomenon, here's proof that it isn't. We intuitively know that pain is in this world because something has gone dreadfully awry. It's not the product of evolutionary processes; it's not a natural part of physical existence; it's aberrant. Life as we know it is not the way it was meant to be. And since sin is fairly easy to see in the behavior of human beings, that sin must be the source of our pain. It makes perfect sense to us that if we have to live with suffering, we must have deserved it.

Of course, we might not agree with the disciples that there is a direct correlation between this individual's blindness and his (or his parents') specific sin. That's too black and white for us moderns to believe, and it's far too politically incorrect. We know things are a little more complex than the disciples' simple assumptions indicate. But we can't be too hard on them, because we hold a very similar belief. We believe that this man was blind because we live in a broken world and that this broken world is a result of original sin. No, we don't believe the correlation is direct, but we do affirm the correlation. All the pain we know about is in this world because our first parents—and we, by genetic predisposition—sinned.

We're a little smug about our interpretation of this passage. We rightly recognize in Jesus's response that he is exposing the disciples' false assumptions. Can we not also see that he is stretching us beyond our assumptions as well? Think about his answer: "It was neither that this man sinned, nor his parents; but it was so that the works of God might be displayed in him" (v. 3 NASB). He clearly denies the disciples their presuppositions. But what about ours?

No, I'm not suggesting that our belief is unbiblical; all the pain that is in this world *really is* a result, directly or indirectly, of our sinful condition. That's a very defensible position, biblically speaking. As much as secular culture tries to convince us that sin has nothing to do with suffering—that sin doesn't even exist, in fact—we aren't convinced, and neither are those who argue that point. We can't relegate evil to fringe psychopaths; we've seen too many news reports for that, and we've even had glimpses into our own hearts. We *know* something is wrong with this world, that it's not in the condition it was intended to be in and that we as human beings have had something to do with that. Even aside from biblical revelation, humanity's inhumanity is painfully obvious. Something has gone horribly wrong, and people suffer from whatever that something is. There's a connection between our rebellion, both internal and external, and the condition in which we find our world.

That, however, is not what Jesus homes in on. He has a golden opportunity here to place the blame of suffering squarely on the shoulders of humanity, where those of us who are theologically sensitive and biblically conservative would agree it rightfully belongs. It was God, after all, who spelled out the curses of disobedience for us back in Genesis, then in Leviticus and Deuteronomy, then through the Prophets, and even to the very end of the book of Revelation. There is definitely, emphatically a connection between the sin of humanity and its pitiful, cursed condition. So when the disciples saw this physically handicapped man and asked Jesus about him, Jesus could have given the conventional, expected response. He easily could have lined up with the weight of Scripture on this issue and told us what we already know: "This is the mess you've gotten yourselves into because you haven't listened to me from the very beginning." He easily could have said, "No, it isn't this man's sin or his parents'; it is simply the by-product of living in a sinful world."

That's what we would have said and, in fact, probably have said at some point in our lives. That fits our theology. Not only that, it's a biblically defensible position. But Jesus squanders this golden opportunity. He takes the burden off the shoulders of man, where the disciples had carefully laid it, and places it on his own! He points to God! He defines this man's suffering as a showcase for the Father.

Look closely. Do you see the cause and effect? "This happened *so that* the work of God might be displayed in his life" (v. 3 NIV). I've heard biblical commentators argue that there is no cause and effect implied in this "so that," but I have never heard them give an alternate interpretation. My guess is that they, like most of us, are wary of attributing evil consequences to God. That's too politically incorrect, too simplistic, too bold. But the structure of the sentence is clear: There is a purpose in this man's blindness. It isn't random, and it isn't even specifically tied to his or anyone else's disobedience. It's all about God being displayed. Yes, there was sin back in the garden, and, yes, there's been ample disobedience since, and, yes, we've suffered because we live in a fallen world. But the biblical text is clear that Jesus completely ignores that particular angle and acknowledges that perhaps God knew about suffering—everyone's, this man's and ours—and permitted it for a reason. No vindication is necessary for this God of love and power; here's a painful situation, and God allowed it—yes, he even set it up—in order to demonstrate his own glory.

Isn't that incredible? We are so careful to blame our brokenness on ourselves; and, indeed, the Bible affirms repeatedly that the sin of our race is what brought on all this suffering. But Jesus doesn't go there. He goes straight to the higher purpose, the higher purpose we wonder about whenever something goes terribly wrong, the higher purpose we tell ourselves isn't there because there are no pat answers in this world, the why of it all. He knows we aren't satisfied to say, "We sinned, and now we suffer. Too bad. That's the sad but necessary result of our free will." He helps us answer this annoying question in the back of our minds about why God went ahead with the plan of his creation when he knew what would happen to it. He says this man's infirmity will point to God's glory, and we are right if we apply the answer more broadly than to physical illness. If this is true—that this blind man's pain is redeemable—then it can be true for all of our infirmities. They can *all* point to his glory. If there is such a clear purpose in this man's blindness, there's a clear hope that we can say the same of ours.

Some might feel that this doesn't exactly vindicate God. We know, theologically, that a holy God *cannot* be the author of evil, nor can he endorse it, nor can he even touch it. But the condition of our world reminds us that evil exists, and the Bible reminds us that God is sovereign. We can argue all we want to about the separation between God and a broken creation, but in the end, if we remain faithful to the biblical witness, we have to conclude that he created this world knowing what would happen to it. We simply can't get around that fact without compromising basic biblical themes. And that, to some degree, ties him to the consequences. It doesn't blame him, and it doesn't make him responsible for evil and suffering, but it does indicate that he is somehow implicitly connected to them. This passage in John 9 indicates that his redemptive nature is glorified by evil's very existence.

Perhaps a little speculation about the blind man's future would help us vindicate God for his role in this world (as though he really needs our defense). After all, if you were the blind man, how would God's purpose for suffering make you feel? Would you resent all those years you had been blind if you knew it would prove a point about God and his greatness? Wouldn't that make God selfish? Wouldn't you feel used and abused?

Human nature, as well as our sophisticated theological arguments, might take us to that perspective, but it won't last long. We have given so much weight to human suffering and so little to God's honor that we might think, for a brief moment, that the pain of this world isn't a fair trade-off. If we hurt so that God can increase his fame, we think twice about the nature of God. For a humanity that magnifies its pain, this seems so beneath a loving Creator.

But how long can we really hold this grudge? Will we be able to maintain it in heaven? When we get there, let's ask this man if those years of blindness on earth were worth an eternally recorded demonstration of the glory of God. What do you think he will say? Do you think he will even take his gaze—yes, his 20/20 gaze—off of his Redeemer for a moment to answer our question? *Worth it?* How could moments of pain come close to outweighing the ultimate value of eternal glory? He traded a few decades of darkness for the pure light of everlasting eons upon eons. Those decades may be just a shadow in his memory. If he does remember them well, the question might make him laugh.

No Pain, No Gain

It should make us laugh too—at ourselves. We will go through all sorts of self-inflicted pain for a thoroughly temporal pleasure: painful diets for the perfect figure, exhausting exercise for greater strength, hard work and long hours for a bigger paycheck, grueling educational regimens for the fast track to a better career—the examples are numerous. "No pain, no gain," we're fond of saying. In fact, one of our greatest joys is related to this principle. Ask any woman in labor if she thinks her baby is going to be worth the pain of the current contraction, and she's likely to claw your eyes out. But if you ask her afterward whether it was worth it, when she's holding the sweet little bundle in her arms, she will look at you with wonder, marveling that any poor, simple fool could even ask such a question. *Of course it was worth it, you idiot,* she'll communicate without a word. The pain was momentary. The result is amazing and forever.

Paul uses this labor metaphor in Romans when he writes about this world groaning for its redemption. Our struggle is a lot like the frightening, blessed event of birth. We hurt now, but there's a payoff later. And for those who believe, the payoff is always greater than the hurt.

So we have no problem fully understanding the concept of momentary sacrifice for long-term benefit, do we? Except when it comes to the ultimate benefit, that is. In the eternal scheme of things, our suffering is extremely momentary, and our gain is extremely long-term. Why is it so difficult to accept? If we embrace this dynamic of inflicting pain on ourselves for much more trivial goals, why, when the God with the eternal perspective allows us to go through pain for the ultimate prize of participating in his glory, do we ask how he could possibly be both loving and powerful? It's a little hypocritical of us. We're as blind as the beggar in Jerusalem.

There's a reason Jesus doesn't mind deflecting the disciples' blame for pain from our sin to his own shoulders. Suffering is entirely justifiable because it can be used for God's glory. That's an utterly shocking revelation to us, surely as shocking as it was to Jesus's disciples. A new premise has been added to the three-pronged problem. Yes, evil exists. Yes, God is loving. Yes, he is omnipotent. How can these three coexist as uncompromised truths? Because there is a higher purpose added to the mix. We can't legitimately consider only those three propositions; we must add a fourth—humanity's role in displaying the glory of God. The skeptics leave out that factor, for obvious reasons; skeptics aren't very concerned about the glory of God. Epicurus left it out because it probably didn't even occur to him. But we who suffer and who want to find meaning in our suffering can find it there. Question number one of the Westminster Shorter Catechism affirms that we exist for God's glory, and it's not a stretch to apply that purpose inclusively to our suffering and pain. We can find no higher meaning to our suffering, in fact. It's incredibly important. It's eternal. And it's worth it.

The "Bless Me" Paradox

A number of years ago, there was a movement in the church—a movement that persists in some circles today—to praise God for who he is rather than for what he can do for us. I understand the sentiment behind that, and I agree with it—in principle. It seems contrary to the gospel to constantly ask God for favors. According to Jesus, we are to deny ourselves and take up our cross daily. A selfish Christianity that centers our prayers entirely around our own interests is opposed to the teachings of Jesus. In theory, we should always praise God for who he is.

There is, however, an insurmountable problem that stands in the way of our putting this into practice. Have you ever tried simply praising God for who he is? What do you say? Perhaps you are able to quote some of the things the Scriptures say—about the character of God, his love, holiness, power, and so on. But how much enthusiasm is behind that praise? For me, not much. I know nothing about that love, holiness, and power in isolation from his works. I've found it impossible to have any concept of who God is apart from what he has done. Furthermore, what he's done is a pretty vague historical concept in my mind unless it is what he has done *for me.*

That's why there is nothing inherently wrong with our approaching God on the basis of our needs. We have to maintain that concept if we're to believe in a God who lets us suffer pain in order, ultimately, to show his own glory. As unattractive as an exclusively "bless me" faith is, there's absolutely nothing in the Bible that tells us there is something wrong with asking God to bless us. Just the opposite is true, in fact. Jesus himself told his disciples to keep on asking, seeking, and knocking, because the Father loves to give good things to his children (Matt. 7:7–10). The Bible is filled to the brim with people in dire situations asking for deliverance, healing, and protection. Read through the Psalms sometime and observe all the declarations of God's greatness; you'll find that such praise is almost all in the context of his doing something concrete in the midst of a psalmist's agonizing crisis. His mercies are not theoretical; they are a revelation of his heart that can come only in the midst of our urgency and pain. In fact, that is the thrust of all of God's revelation; he's the rescuer God who is known only—or at least primarily—in the context of human need. We are therefore negligent for *not* praying those prayers for blessing. Need is the impetus that moves our praise of God from abstract theory to concrete faith and gratitude. The human experience is that ordained stage for those formerly hidden divine attributes to be displayed.

Think about that. Ask yourself what you know of God personally and how you got that knowledge. In my experience, nearly everything I know of God was discovered in the context of my spiritual, physical, emotional, or psychological poverty. And I'm pretty sure my experience is not very unusual. We do not experience him—really know him—until we are desperate and he delivers. It is therefore perfectly all right to ask God to bless us. In fact, it is required. He is a blesser by nature; his nature remains hidden if we do not appeal to him for help.

If you're still wondering just how scriptural this concept is, think of the names God gives himself: Jehovah-Jireh, Provider; Jehovah-Rapha, Healer; Jehovah-Nissi, Banner (in victory). Read how often he reminds the Israelites that he is the God who delivered them. He is remarkably redundant about it. Remember his ultimate revelation to Moses: "The LORD, the LORD, a God merciful and gracious, slow to anger, and abounding in steadfast love and faithfulness, keeping steadfast love for thousands, forgiving iniquity and transgression and sin" (Exod. 34:6–7). What, in all of these names and descriptions, does not also imply our suffering? Very little. Our prayers for blessing appeal to this God, and these merciful, rescuing characteristics of his are the main emphasis of who he is in Scripture. Asking the Blesser to bless us is by no means inappropriate.

The problem that critics of "bless me" Christianity really mean to target is our shallow understanding and unrealistic expectations of what a blessing actually is. We often want God to follow our own agenda rather than his better agenda. Our agenda does not include the essential, primary elements of relationship, character development, Christlikeness, and other forms of spiritual growth. We are usually not eternally focused in our vision of God's deliverance. We don't see the big picture of how his blessing will glorify him; we focus, rather, on how his blessing will benefit us. We just want God to save our skin, provide some material gift, elevate our status, or grant some other shortsighted goal. We ask him for things, positions, or circumstances that will help us feel secure, comfortable, or victorious. What we really desire is the security, comfort, or victory we think the things, positions, or circumstances will give us.

That's why God's answers to our prayers often look so different from how we envisioned them. He's all for our security, comfort, and victory; he just disagrees with our means of getting them, so he provides a deeper, more genuine means. But he never tells us not to ask for the blessing. A "bless me" prayer is almost always appropriate, especially if we understand the ultimate purpose behind his answer. We just have to learn what his blessing looks like and to know what we're really asking—and why we're asking it.

We also have to learn to pray things other than "bless me." That is legitimate as an integral part of our prayer life, but it cannot be its entirety. When it is, we are self-centered and offensive to those around us. There is a huge difference between praying, "Lord, bless me so I can have what I want," and "Lord, bless me so you can be glorified." The latter prayer understands prayer's purpose; the former often has no interest in God. It can seem like an incantation or a magic spell.

A full, mature understanding of prayer knows that God is to be experienced in the context of our neediness, and it does not hesitate to bang on the door of heaven (see Luke 11:5–10) for the riches of God to be poured out. But it does understand that the ultimate purpose of that request is to bring glory to God, to demonstrate the blessing nature of the blesser God. Knowing that his answers to our prayers will indeed bless us and benefit us in a multitude of ways, we must nevertheless ask for deliverance to display the rescuer God, for providence to display the provider God, and for healing to display the healer God. As John Piper is fond of saying, God is most glorified in us when we are most satisfied in him. That implies that we will be delivered, healed, and supplied—or entirely content in our knowledge of God when his intervention is delayed or obscured or even withheld for a time.

We must remember that while we feel like we have much at stake when we pray for God's help, he has much at stake as well. Scripture is all about his demonstrating his character and his ways; he is still intensely interested in demonstrating himself in the lives of his people today.

If you have been convinced that your prayers for blessing are selfish, ask yourself why. Have you been asking with entirely selfish motives, using God as your spiritual Santa Claus, only to dispense with him after you've got what you want? Then your convictions about your prayers are correct. But if you're asking him to bless you because you know that's what he does by his very nature, both to benefit you and to glorify himself, then dispense with the false guilt. We do not need to feel guilty about asking for God's favor. We are urged to ask him for his goodness. We must dig deeper than our commonly superficial prayers in order to ask him this in the right spirit. But we can know that God means to reveal himself in our lives and that his revelation comes in the context of our deep need—even when that need is self-inflicted by sin. That's what our desperate situation in this fallen world is all about: the God of blessing showing up. That fact can give our darkest hours and our sharpest pains some semblance of meaning.

6

The Centerpiece of the Universe

All things have been created through Him and for Him.

Colossians 1:16 NASB

Try an experiment: Pick an evening—any evening of the week—and watch one channel on your TV. Every time a commercial comes on, briefly summarize its theme on a notepad. At the end of the evening, read the notes you've taken. You'll probably find some interesting trends. You'll find promises of fulfillment if you'll drive this or that car. You'll find assurances that the key to picking up that right mate (or temporary partner) is found in your makeup, your clothing, your toothpaste, or the beer you drink. You'll find that the right appliances will make your life *so* much easier. You'll find that true happiness comes from financial security, which comes from the right investment plan or the right amount of insurance coverage. You'll find whatever you need to be in good hands, to go for the gusto, to let yourself go, or to get a break today (which, by the way, you deserve). In other words, you'll find that it's all about you.

Far too often we have a human-centered view of the universe. Our culture indoctrinates us thoroughly in this perspective. We see creation as something God made for our sake, not his, and we struggle to see why pain is a necessary part of our well-being. When we pray for God to heal us, deliver us, or otherwise bless us, we think we're the only ones with something at stake in the request. We think it's all about us, that our existence is a desirable end in itself, not an existence that points to a greater purpose. If our existence were the ultimate goal, then our well-being would be the ultimate good. Our comfort would serve that goal, and pain and evil would be pieces of a puzzle that simply would not fit. None of it would make sense.

Popular secular religion—that amorphous sentiment that God is up there and tolerates everything we do—has, in fact, taken that course. In that worldview in which our well-being is the ultimate good, self-fulfillment alone fits the puzzle. We call it by a variety of terms: the quest to reach human potential, self-actualization, the next step in human evolution, and so on. A semblance of heaven can fit this picture too, but not hell. God quickly becomes an aide to our development as mature human beings—our divine butler, so to speak. He will help us reach fulfillment and get to heaven.

That derives from the Christian perspective, but it's not quite accurate. It's a little too me-oriented to be completely biblical. If our focus is entirely on our growth, with God as a means to our ultimate end, we have a distorted view. The result is that when we see all the suffering we and others experience, we intuitively know that this is not how things should be, and we come up with explanations as to why we're at fault or why God allows suffering, as though our suffering were really all about us.

While we are certainly participants, our suffering is not all about us. It is about God. We know this because everything in the universe is ultimately about God. We are not the center of anything; he is the center of everything. That is why when we cry out in our anguish, "God, why are you doing this to me?" we are revealing our lowly frame of reference. We're forgetting we exist for him, not him for us. We're showing a natural inclination to think our well-being is the ultimate good, and since this pain doesn't fit with our understanding of what is good, we're confused. A better question would be, "God, how do you want to reveal yourself in this situation?" It makes more sense to consider God's ultimate purpose in demonstrating his character. That may be completely unnatural to our fallen state, but it is more appropriate.

So a natural starting point for discussing the problem of evil should focus on God's purposes for his good, or even our purposes for his good, but not his purposes for our good. (His purposes for our good are, in fact, relevant, but they aren't our—or the Bible's—starting point.) There is, of course, no inherent contradiction between what is good for God and what is good for those who love him, but our emphasis must be on the former if we are to rightly understand things. This universe was created first and foremost for God's purposes through the Son—numerous passages say so (Eph. 1:11–12 and Col. 1:16, for two examples among many)—and everything must be seen in that light. When we ask why we must suffer in some situation, we must be careful not to imply that we think the universe revolves around us.

What does it revolve around? There is no higher value than God's glory. That is, according to logic and the Bible, the centerpiece of the universe. All things will either point to it or be judged. If God is omniscient, omnipotent, infinitely wise, infinitely beautiful, radiant in his very existence, then the highest value we can hold is him—or, as he is manifested to us, his glory. There is nothing higher.

Glory: What Is It?

"The glory of God." It sounds like a trite religious phrase, doesn't it? It's hard to get a handle on for several reasons, one being the pious nature of the verbiage. The problem is that we don't have many other ways of expressing the concept. His glory can mean his fame, his reputation, his honor, and his greatness, but it's more than that. It involves his beauty and our adulation. It's whatever of God shines visibly for us and the rest of creation to see. In some senses it's abstract, but it will not always be. That's what heaven will be about: taking in all the glory we can handle. We will be overwhelmed by his greatness and the honor we owe him.

But is God's glory really all it's cracked up to be? Can we really build our perspective on something so abstract? Whether we can conceive of his glory or not, we have to revolve around it, because that's what the Bible says all creation revolves around. We cannot come up with another goal that would even come close to rivaling the glory of God in significance. Try putting it in human terms of glory—honor and attention that come with human achievement. Would winning an Olympic gold medal compare to the glory due to God? Hardly. A national championship? Please. Touching the whole world with a profound but human-centered musical masterpiece or work of art? That's nothing compared to displaying his glory. At the center of this universe burns an intensely bright, worthy, magnificent, driving purpose, and it's more than we can imagine, so we use an entirely religious and insufficient term for it. *Glory*. It's all we have.

Think about how the biblical emphasis on glory translates to our own lives. There is no accolade, no achievement, no possession comparable to this ultimate treasure. Our earthly ambitions cost us much sacrifice—that "no pain, no gain" philosophy again—and the glory of God will cost us much sacrifice too. There's a lot of pain with the gain. But the confidence of an inspired Paul is emphatic: "I consider that the sufferings of this present time are not worth comparing with the glory that is to be revealed to us" (Rom. 8:18). The revelation of God's glory is paramount; everything—even evil, even universal suffering, even our individual pain—exists for that purpose.

Even a cursory reading of the Bible would indicate to us that all God does points toward his glory. He chose Abraham to establish a nation that would bring *honor to his name* among all nations. He answered Moses's prayer to preserve his rebellious people *for the glory of his name*. He strengthened David against the ominous Goliath *for the glory of his name*. Jesus prayed that the disciples would bear fruit *for the glory of his name*. These are not implied inferences; they are specified in the relevant texts, and the examples are nearly limitless. "The heavens declare the glory of God, and the sky above proclaims his handiwork" (Ps. 19:1). So should we.

John Piper has written much about God being "uppermost in his own affections."[1] In us, of course, this attitude would be arrogance, simply because it is an overestimation of our own worth. We should never be uppermost in our own affections. But with God, there can be no overestimation of value. God prizes his own glory because there is nothing higher to prize. It isn't conceit; it's realism. Piper gives extensive biblical evidence that "God's ultimate goal in all he does is to preserve and display his glory."[2] The belief that God created a world that would fall specifically as a means to display his merciful character is simply a logical conclusion from this fact that his glory is the worthiest of all goals for him and for us.[3]

There should be no great mystery to the presence of evil if, by context and by contrast, it reveals the manifold character of God. The highest value is always worth lesser costs. And, according to the Bible, suffering is *always* a lesser cost.

The Potter's Prerogative

A common scriptural image of the Creator's relationship to the created is the potter's relationship to the clay. Isaiah uses it, and so does Paul. It is particularly relevant to this problem of suffering. "Will what is molded say to its molder, 'Why have you made me like this?'" Paul writes in Romans 9:20–23. "Has the potter no right over the clay? . . . What if God, desiring to show his wrath and to make known his power, has endured with much patience vessels of wrath prepared for destruction, in order to make known the riches of his glory for vessels of mercy, which he has prepared beforehand for glory." This argument in Romans pertains to salvation and the doctrine of election, but we might ask the same sort of questions as to why we—either individually or collectively as a people—were chosen as vessels for suffering. Paul's conclusion with regard to judgment and wrath—and, by implication, to any type of suffering—is that God's choice of vessels is justified if it leads to a demonstration of his glory.

Consider the lowly lump of clay. Suppose the clay on the potter's wheel could talk to the artist handling it. If the clay were to cry out, "Why are you doing this to me? Don't you know how painful this is? Don't you know that every time you knead me, tear off a piece of me, slather me in water, gouge me with your tools, hollow out my middle, and fire me in your kiln, you are hurting me?" wouldn't we consider this a very clay-centered perspective? Surely there's more going on here than the comfort of the clay.

The process isn't about the clay at all, at least not the clay in itself. It's about what the artist can do with the clay. The clay is certainly a participant in the process; in fact, it's quite intensely involved. But its feelings aren't the predominant issue. And if the clay could see the end result, it might even be glad for the process, however painful it is. It would know that it exists for the potter's glory and not vice versa. It is not there for the sake of clayness. Clay-fulfillment is not its legitimate aspiration. The clay exists to eventually reveal something of the mind of its shaper.

The ultimate good in this scenario would involve artistry, technique, use of color, form and function, and the like—in other words, the wisdom and vision of the potter, not the pleasure of the clay. The clay's comfort would be a peripheral issue, because the final product on display would be a welcome reality. The clay's pain gives way to its own beauty, which it could not have foreseen, and to the potter's glory in making it. It's an entirely reasonable pain.

And that's our promise—that our pain will be reasonable and the finished product will be beautiful. There's purpose in it. In the midst of all of his distresses and persecutions, Paul gives us this word of hope, the promise to which we cling in the midst of our suffering: "This light momentary affliction is preparing for us an eternal weight of glory beyond all comparison" (2 Cor. 4:17). Our troubles do not seem light and momentary when we are going through them, but, in the eternal scheme of things, they are. The glory to which Paul points belongs to God, but, as the verse makes clear, it is shared with us (a point that will be developed later). The glory of the Potter will be reflected in the pottery. "The sufferings of this present time are not worth comparing with the glory that is to be revealed to us" (Rom. 8:18).

Meanwhile, "we groan, longing to put on our heavenly dwelling" (2 Cor. 5:2). It's the groan of all creation, a creation that is frustrated and decaying but that knows a revelation of glory is coming (Rom. 8:18–25). The suffering and groaning, according to Paul and the testimony of the rest of Scripture, will be worth it.

How does this help us in the here and now? When we see ourselves as material in the service of the Potter's hand, we begin to see suffering differently. A lump of clay on the potter's shelf might strive all it can for self-fulfillment, but it would be an exercise in futility. It is there for noble purposes, but it becomes noble only when the artist has his way. Without the potter, it will never be anything other than the grayish-brown color it is. It will never change shape, other than its slight degradation due to environmental elements. In short, it can do nothing worthwhile in itself. It is entirely frustrated if it expects otherwise. But it is immensely worthwhile to the potter, both for its current substance and for its breathtaking potential. It exists for the artist's glory, and its value was crafted into it to demonstrate something about the artist that others can observe and appreciate.

That's us, as much as we hate to admit it. In all of our efforts at self-improvement, we may change ever so slightly, but we never change to anything substantially better than what we were. But in the Potter's hands, we can become works of art. If we can trust those hands to do their work, even when it hurts, we may be able to get a glimpse of the Potter's purposes in ways we would never see if we remained on the shelf. We would actually get to know the Potter himself, and that would be an infinitely greater good, worth every moment of pain on the wheel. In short, we would see glory, and so would all who visited the Potter's museum. His artistry, his splendor, would be displayed for all.

Is your pain worth that? Perhaps a better question would be, Is there anything that isn't worth that?

An Olympian Pursuit

The race is about to begin, but first the network commentators give us an in-depth feature on the athlete who is about to compete. She has been training for fifteen long years—since she was seven. Every morning before school, she would get up and swim laps for two hours. Every afternoon after school, she would go back to the pool and swim laps for three more hours. Her diet has been strictly regulated—by her coaches and her own willpower—for as long as she can remember. She has been able to participate in some normal high school activities, but not many. Most of her free time has been spent in training. She has suffered sore muscles, worked herself to exhaustion, and trained in spite of injuries. She's a model of discipline and self-denial. Her eyes have been focused on the goal for practically her whole life. She wants to win gold.

The story is a composite of nearly every athlete who has ever competed at that level in any sport. We're quite familiar with the concept of self-denial for a greater gain. An athlete in training denies his urges and impulses. When he needs a break and wants to sleep in, he says no. When his friends ask him to parties and activities that would interfere with his training, he says no. When his parents have money to spend on either a larger house or one of the world's premier coaches, they choose the coach. He and those who love him suffer for the ultimate goal.

The day comes when the athlete competes at the highest level. There has been no widespread recognition until then.

Only when the cameras are on and the world is watching will winning a medal be widely applauded. Even then, it has all been a risk. Only a few athletes out of the multitude who have followed the rigorous training regimen for all those years will even compete, much less place high enough for a medal. But the risk is considered worthwhile for these athletes. Extraordinary sacrifice is a small price to pay for the honor to be gained.

The athlete voluntarily suffers now for the sake of future glory. Think of our culture's many expressions of this theme. I have a lot of experience with this, and you probably do as well. I've pinched pennies and embraced radical austerity at various times in order to save for a much-needed vacation, an education, a new car, and many other purchases. I joined a gym recently, so I stress and strain and grunt and groan to work off the tragedy of my fortysomething midsection. I've spent long hours in prayer, Bible study, and fasting just to experience something deeper of God's will and his character. You can probably identify with some of these things. But what do we say when we're told we suffer pain in order for God to reveal something of his nature? *That's not fair!*

Why isn't it fair? We normally have no problem with no pain, no gain; we even honor it, as in the case of the athlete, with our highest admiration, profuse media attention, and extravagant corporate sponsorships. Our problem comes when the sacrifice and the suffering are chosen *for* us rather than *by* us. If we choose self-denial and discomfort for future gain, we think we choose nobly and wisely. After all, Jesus did that: Hebrews 12:2 tells us he endured the cross for the joy that would come later. But if we are to deny ourselves and suffer for a future glory, we want to make sure that we choose the suffering and that the future glory will be ours. We're offended when such sacrifice is imposed against our will. An athlete whose parents forced rigorous training on him may resent it. We don't like involuntary sacrifice. We feel as if our rights have been violated.

This, however, is exactly the dynamic God places on us. We suffer now for his future glory—a glory that we are blessed to participate in, if we will. Our natural, sinful selves don't like that. We complain about the hardship we have to go through. Such complaining seems entirely appropriate to us, especially when the hardship is severe. That's understandable, given our earthly point of view. The consistent witness of the Bible, however, is that looking back on it, we will affirm that the future glory was worth the past costs. We can, like the early apostles, rejoice that we have been "considered worthy to suffer shame for His name" (Acts 5:41 NASB). Or, in a more general sense of suffering, we are counted worthy to suffer for a greater revelation of him. We're assured that the final revelation of God in this earthly scene will be unimaginably glorious. His splendor will far outweigh any pain we experience now. One day it will all make sense.

Meanwhile, when we lack, we complain, just as the Israelites did in the wilderness. We aren't aware that we would gladly impose our suffering on ourselves if only we knew the future blessing, just as the athlete has his eye on the gold and the honor. But if it is imposed on us from above, will we trust the Almighty to make that decision for us? The all-wise, all-knowing God sees the current trial *and* the end result, and he decides on our behalf that the current trial is worth it. We see only the trial, and we wonder. Do we really have any reason to trust our assessment of the situation over God's?

We need to have the attitude of the athlete, but with a God-centered rather than self-centered perspective. The suggestion that God might let us suffer for his honor rubs us the wrong way, but nothing bothers us about the illustration of the self-imposed sacrifices of the athlete. Our admiration for people who are dedicated to a worthwhile goal that requires exhaustion and pain for the moment must be accepted of ourselves. We can no longer criticize the Creator for our pain when we understand that we are promised a goal infinitely more worthwhile than gold medals and endorsement contracts.

This is a principle we must learn to trust: God's assessment of what constitutes a worthwhile goal is far more accurate than ours. Paul compares himself to a runner who is competing not for a perishable wreath but for an imperishable one (1 Cor. 9:24–27). We must repeatedly remind ourselves that God's glory is infinitely greater than a gold medal, a World Series ring, or a Super Bowl trophy. The medals, rings, and trophies are made of earthly elements that will eventually degrade, as all physical elements do. Long before they degrade, they will be stuck in some box of keepsakes or put on some dust-prone shelf. Or maybe they will be encased in glass in some quiet corner of a museum. The newspaper articles will turn brown and brittle. The praises will die down, and only a handful of true sports enthusiasts will remember what happened way back at the Olympics or league championships so many years ago. And the athletes' bodies, having reached their peak, will enter a steady decline from age and atrophy, never to repeat that one brief shining moment. Human glory fades.

God's glory doesn't fade. It's eternal. The honor we bring to him in the crucible of life will stand as a trophy forever. The character he reveals to us in our deepest trials will give us glimpses of the unfathomable Almighty that many earthbound creatures will perhaps never see. Though the pain of this world is agonizing and devastating, the costs of experiencing it still can never outweigh the benefits of the glory he reveals about himself or the glory of the character he develops in us. We get a strong sense in the Bible that if we saw the end result, we would tolerate much more of the means of displaying it. Why? Because we, by the work of God in our hearts, become partakers of his glory. He shares it with us! Can the pain of temporal suffering even compare to the priceless worth of such a gift?

7

Out of Egypt, Into Glory

The Scripture says to Pharaoh, "For this very purpose I have raised you up, that I might show my power in you, and that my name might be proclaimed in all the earth."

Romans 9:17

Imagine being a Middle Eastern slave in about 1500 BC. Slavery is all you've ever known. You've heard of ancestors from four hundred years earlier who lived in a privileged position, but for generations—too long to hope that the situation is temporary—your people have been subjugated by a stronger, unsympathetic race. Their great achievements are accomplished by your strength and sweat. Your children are not allowed to dream of what they will accomplish one day, because you know they will be pawns of the sons of your oppressors. They will spend their days in the hot Egyptian sun just like you do. And, just like you, they will spend their evenings listening to the recitation of oral traditions of how you came to be in this place.

This is a noble history, but you've fallen in status. Your traditions even tell of prophecies of deliverance—one of them says your captivity will last only four hundred years. Only four hundred? What an unfathomably long time to suffer. Generations have passed never knowing freedom. From the looks of things, so will yours. There's no sign of deliverance. The prophecy of the four hundred years must have been wishful thinking. Come to think of it, so must the God who is said to have inspired that prophecy. Where is he? If he cares at all, why hasn't he intervened? Why does he let the suffering continue?

This, of course, is the context of the exodus. For more than four centuries, the descendants of Abraham, Isaac, and Jacob lived in this place. By the providence of God, they came to Egypt to avoid famine. Through Joseph's captivity at the hands of his brothers, God made a way for them to thrive in a land of plenty. But after Joseph's death, they fell out of favor. Didn't God see this coming? Why did God's providence turn into such disaster? Why did something intended as a blessing for Joseph's family become the vehicle for a brutal, hopeless captivity? Why did God's people have to suffer?

The slavery that preceded the exodus is an apt illustration of the entire human condition. It was long-lasting—seemingly permanent to the generations not fortunate enough to have lived at either end of the four hundred plus years. It was painful: "The Egyptians were in dread of the people of Israel. So they ruthlessly made the people of Israel work as slaves and made their lives bitter with hard service" (Exod. 1:12–14). The questions we ask today about the pain and suffering in the world are likely the same ones the Israelites asked in their captivity. We have a very similar line of reasoning. Where we ask why evil is allowed to exist, they asked why the Egyptians were allowed to hold them as slaves. Both we and they have asked, "How long, Lord?" And when that answer doesn't come quickly, we've asked, "Where are you, Lord?"

The exodus event is a microcosm of our world and God's activity in it. There is captivity, there is evil, and there is hopelessness. But there is also a God who steps into that hopelessness with mercy and deliverance. But why did God allow four centuries of captivity before stepping in?

To Hollywood, the exodus is a good plot for epic films. But to Judaism, it is the landmark event in the history of Israel; and to Christianity, it is the great foreshadowing of our deliverance from sin and death, a picture of eternal salvation. An enslaved people was delivered at the prophesied time by the hand of God through the man Moses. Through a series of plagues that were an assault on Egyptian pride and an affront to national deities, Pharaoh was convinced to let the Hebrews go. Regretting the decision, Pharaoh and his army pursued them to the edge of the Red Sea, which miraculously opened long enough to let the Hebrews through but not long enough to let the pursuers through. With the Promised Land ahead, God led his people through the wilderness by a cloud and fire, fed them with manna from heaven, gave them the law to govern their society and their relationship with him, and judged them when they rebelled against him. All the while, he was very clear about one thing: he wanted to be known.

God could have chosen to reveal himself in a vacuum—that is, with no context for his actions—but the revelation would have fallen on unperceiving subjects. God could have simply spoken from heaven: "I am merciful. I am compassionate. I am your Redeemer, your Healer, and your Provider." But outside the context of sin, captivity, and sickness, there would be no point. These words would mean nothing. There had to be a stage, a plot, and an audience. The mercies of God, infinitely valuable, had to have a meaningful expression.

But anyone looking only at a small snapshot of the experience —the slavery in Egypt, the pursuit of the Egyptian army, the wanderings in the wilderness, the hunger and thirst—without the larger picture of God's wonderful intervention would complain about God's lack of concern, or even about his nonexistence. In fact, that's exactly what many of the Israelites did in the wilderness—they looked at snapshots of suffering without retaining knowledge of the big picture.

And that's exactly what we do. We see the misery of suffering humanity with limited vision, unaware (and perhaps uninterested) that there is a God who offers himself as Comforter to the brokenhearted, as Defender to the defenseless, and ultimately as Savior to all who are lost and will come to him. We home in on the negatives and forget that there is a revelation of an overwhelmingly merciful Lord who has promised to make all things right for those who trust him on his terms. Our restricted point of view lets us see the stage and its props without understanding the plot. We've read the middle acts while ignoring the introduction and the conclusion.

The exodus paints a clear picture of a God who has allowed a horrifying situation in order to step into it. The testimony of the Mosaic books shows us God as an intensely involved, interested, mighty participant in the human condition. He is not absent, and he is not unconcerned with our pain. Though he let it continue for four centuries under Egyptian rule, he did so for a purpose—that at the appropriate time, he might step in, show himself, and establish his people as an act of mercy.

But there were conditions that gave God's revelation meaning: captivity and slavery in Egypt, oppression by the captors, the hard-heartedness of Pharaoh, the poverty of the

Israelites, the very real danger at the edge of the sea, the surrounding context of ungodliness, and the lack of resources in the wilderness. God became their Deliverer, their Defender, their holy Lawgiver, their Provider, and everything else he became, only because they needed deliverance, defense, holiness, providence, and a number of other helps. The uncomfortable context, full of suffering and pain, was the vehicle by which they came face-to-face with their Creator and saw him in his glory. This was of such value that the cost of their initial suffering could not compare.

So it was that deliverance from their slavery in Egypt became the most commemorated event in all of Hebrew history, the subject of psalms and celebrations for centuries thereafter. In every trial and tribulation that came later, the Israelites appealed to what they knew to be God's character—knowledge that was forged in the painful sufferings of Egypt and the barren wilderness of Sinai. "So you led your people, to make for yourself a glorious name" (Isa. 63:14).

Is it discomforting that God would allow misery in order to show himself strong? As much as we blame all suffering on our own sinful condition—rightly, since God is not the author of evil—God claims responsibility for letting it happen. He sometimes even makes himself out to be the active agent (Rom. 9:17, for example), an aspect of Scripture we often have trouble with because it doesn't fit into the logic of our theologies. God let Joseph be sold into slavery in order to deliver his chosen family into Egypt, he ordained centuries of slavery, and he hardened Pharaoh's heart, setting up a desperate situation. Then he led his people into the wilderness, deprived them of food and water, and exposed them to scorpions and snakes—*all for a redemptive purpose!*

That's why the biblical writers have no qualms about pointing out that hardship occurs under God's sovereignty and even under his directive hand. Deuteronomy 8 is perhaps the clearest example of this: God led his people into the desert to humble them and test them, "causing [them] to hunger and then feeding [them] with manna" (v. 3 NIV), all to highlight their dependence on him. That verse on a grander scale is the dynamic of all of fallen creation. God caused us to hunger and then fed us with manna. Why? So that we would know him.

If God did this on a national scale for Israel, why wouldn't it be plausible that he has done the same thing on a global scale for the human race? Does he exhibit one personality for the micro-history of a nation and a different personality for the macro-history of the world? If all of Israel's misery and suffering was ordained for a redemptive purpose, even if it included the nonredemptive suffering of many Egyptians for the sake of his glory, isn't this a principle that also makes sense when applied to the whole of creation?

Whether this fits philosophical worldviews or not, it is biblically indisputable that God allowed the suffering of many to (1) display his own glory and (2) let some of his creation witness and enjoy his merciful acts. He set the stage for his own show.

The Glory Priority

> Bring my sons from afar and my daughters from the end of the earth, everyone who is called by my name, whom I created for my glory.
>
> Isaiah 43:6–7

Gideon went to battle against the Midianites with thirty-two thousand men. It seemed like a good idea. He had checked out his authority to do so with great tentativeness and a couple of fleece tests, and God had given him the go-ahead. But then God said no—not to the battle but to the strength of the army. He told Gideon he had too many men!

Is our great Warrior a little deficient in his understanding of good military strategy? Why would God do such a thing, sending men away from the battle? Because the glory was to be his, not Israel's. He whittled the forces down to a mere three hundred. It had to be a clearly divine victory, not a human achievement.

We distort our successes by calling them ours. That's what human pride is all about. We understand the concept of desiring glory—we crave it and strive for it all our lives. The problem is that our glory is misplaced. We've never had a success, a victory, or an achievement that was not given to us, either directly or through the resources we used. There is no such thing as a self-made man. Glory can be demonstrated both in our successes and in our sufferings, and it belongs to God. We were brought into existence to demonstrate that.

The Bible is full of examples of God taking our barrenness, weakness, infirmity, sin, and all other sorts of frailties and bringing honor to himself through them. One of my favorite examples is in 2 Chronicles 20, when Jehoshaphat is surrounded by a vast army from a hostile coalition. God honors Jehoshaphat's response: "We are powerless against this great horde that is coming against us. We do not know what to do, but our eyes are on you" (v. 12). As always in the human story, God carries the weight of deliverance upon himself: "Stand firm, hold your position, and see the salvation of the LORD on your behalf" (v. 17). So Jehoshaphat appointed people to go out in front of the army singing praises to God for the splendor of his holiness. Their praises prompted the Warrior to action; he caused the invading forces to set ambushes against each other.

What is so remarkable about this story? It's that God is able to show himself in the weaknesses and brokenness of human beings. This is particularly applicable to our suffering. Our need brings us to him with cries of dependence. That is exactly how he would have liked for us to relate to him all along: as dependents. He doesn't reluctantly step in to help us when we're down; he delights in the opportunity. When we win our own victories, overcome our own suffering, and persevere in our own strength, we glorify ourselves. When we cry out to him with a proper understanding of who he is and how he saves us, he glorifies himself.

Our confessions teach this, don't they? The Westminster Shorter Catechism asserts that "the chief end of man is to glorify God and enjoy him forever." That's the answer to the great philosophical question, Why are we here? We're here to glorify God. That's our primary purpose. Everything else is secondary.

When we really begin to understand this, our suffering becomes much less of a mystery and much more of an honor. Our suffering, just like our existence, is not primarily about us but about him. I can interpret my pain as beneficial to me in a number of ways without ever really understanding why it's there to begin with. I see profitable side effects but no overarching purpose.

But if I see my pain as something for God's purposes, my eyes open up to a whole host of possibilities. I don't have to know how he glorifies himself in my pain, just that he does. Perhaps he wants to show mercy in it. Perhaps he wants to deliver me from it, showing off his supernatural powers. Perhaps he wants to demonstrate how he helps his people persevere. Maybe it's to demonstrate a godly patience, or to show his power in my weakness, or to equip me to minister to other sufferers. The possibilities are nearly limitless. *But they are all about him!*

That's basically the premise of this book. The Bible emphasizes the preeminence of the glory of God. It is the obsession of psalmists and prophets and apostles. Paul would have gladly died to highlight the glory of Jesus (Phil. 1:20–21). Many of the early disciples did. In parts of the world, many still do. If you've ever wondered what your salvation is really about, read Ephesians 1. We might have thought it was just about getting us to heaven, but there's a higher purpose than that wonderful side effect. Our salvation is not primarily about us. Ephesians 1 is clear: It is "to the praise of his glorious grace" (v. 6); "to the praise of his glory" (v. 12); and "to the praise of his glory" again (v. 14). Ephesians 2:1–10 begins with our depravity and ends with the grace that is a gift; it includes the assertion that we were raised with Christ "so that in the ages to come [God] might show the surpassing riches of His grace" (v. 7 NASB). In spite of our natural tendency to think otherwise, it's not really about us. Everything in all creation is to honor the Creator. It's all about God.

Understanding this requires a radical reorientation of our minds. They are to be renewed so that we willingly offer our bodies as living sacrifices, which is our essential act of worship (Rom. 12:1–2). We are to become decisively God-centered.

For all of us who are steeped in self-centeredness—a universal malady among members of the fallen race—becoming radically God-centered is a shock to the system. We no longer make decisions based on what seems best for us; we make them based on what seems best for God and his kingdom and his truth. We no longer plan our lives; we let him plan them according to his perfect will. We no longer obey our own whims and lusts; we obey his Word. And if we really want to take this to its logical conclusion, we no longer suffer for ourselves, but we suffer for him. We begin to understand our pain as his domain, used for his purposes, existing to demonstrate something about him. The most high God is more clearly glorified, more relevant and visible, in our depths.

A Window to God

The existence of evil can actually serve as a window into the heart of God. It isn't that there's evil in his heart; that's not even remotely true. But, as we have clearly seen, he has allowed it, and he's a rational God. Surely the reason for evil must tell us something about him—about how he works, what he desires, what his motives for this world are, and, consequently, what his motives are for you and me individually. It tells us that he wants to be known by us and through us, even if the costs are high.

This fact—that God's desire is to be known not just in general but also in our own personal trials and temptations—is enormously comforting. We have a hard time suffering for no apparent reason; the seeming senselessness bothers us. But when we suffer and believe God has allowed it for a reason, we are encouraged. We are even motivated to endure. If he wants to be known, we want to know him. That's an honor. Our pain turns into privilege, the emblem of a highly favored child. It's up to us to find out *how* God wants to be known in our pain, although we can certainly ask him for understanding. But we can know that there's always something of God to be discovered when we hurt—his comfort, his power, his love, his healing, his deliverance, *something*. Regardless of the particular attribute he wants to reveal, if he wants to be seen and experienced in the context of our fallen condition—yours, mine, everyone's—we truly have a high calling. It doesn't matter that the costs are high; the benefits will always outweigh them.

8

The Fellowship of the Sufferers

The name of the second he called Ephraim, "For God has made me fruitful in the land of my affliction."

Genesis 41:52

It begins matter-of-factly. "A psalm of David, when he fled from Absalom his son." That's the biblical reference to the context of Psalm 3, which is one of my favorites. David writes of God being his shield, his glory, and the "lifter" of his head (v. 3). I've thought about this psalm in the middle of the night when I can't go back to sleep. "I lay down and slept," David says. "I woke again, for the LORD sustained me" (v. 5). David overcame fear in this psalm, even when surrounded by thousands of adversaries. I may not have thousands of adversaries, but I often feel like I do. I learn something about God in this psalm, and the only reason I learn it is because of when it was written. David wrote it when his foes were many and people were saying he had no salvation in God. He wrote it when he was hurting.

It is no coincidence that so many of the psalms begin with deep distress and end with extravagant praise. David's and the other psalmists' laments almost always begin with crisis, but a victorious God—or at least a triumphant faith in him—shows up in nearly every one. Even when the suffering is self-inflicted, as it always is when we've sinned ourselves into a corner, the outcome can be God honoring. Take David's confession in Psalm 51:14, for example. "Deliver me from bloodguiltiness, O God, O God of my salvation, and my tongue will sing aloud of your righteousness." There's beauty in forgiveness, but you can see it only in a broken world. Perfection precludes it. Such praises in response to restoration just aren't offered when all is well. God's mercy isn't seen in purity.

It doesn't take much Bible reading to realize a distinct trend: God's people suffer. We've already explored why that is; we suffer because we can't experience his mercies if we don't. If God's revelation of himself in this world is about all his comforting attributes, then it only makes sense that the people through whom he reveals himself will be extremely needy for such comfort. That's God's modus operandi in this world: choose some people, let them suffer, let them cry out, meet their need.

We see that from the earliest pages of Scripture. Abraham had been promised an heir, so he waited. And waited. And waited. Then God delivered on his promise, demonstrating his miraculous, unexpected power along with his touch of grace. Then he asked for the most excruciating of sacrifices: the promised child on the altar. Abraham had already been through the pain of longing and the pain of perseverance. Now he would go through the pain of sacrifice. Then God delivered. We, along with Jews and Muslims, call Abraham the father of our faith, because he demonstrated faith in the midst of a lot of suffering.

God glorified himself in the life of Jeremiah, the weeping prophet whose life was full of sorrow. Jeremiah wished he had never been born. He had more enemies than he could count, he constantly delivered bad news, and he was cast into a pit for telling the truth. All of his suffering came because he was obedient. Where's the glory in that? Jeremiah has been an inspiration to every generation since, all because he suffered for the character of God. And God vindicated him in the end.

The apostles demonstrated the glory priority too. They rejoiced that they could suffer for his name (Acts 5:41). Paul was completely reckless when it came to his own pain, always focusing it on God in one way or another. Peter reminded his readers that their trials were temporary and the glory to follow was imperishable. James encouraged his readers to consider their trials pure joy—a wholly unnatural reaction for us, but the appropriate one. If we only knew the weight of glory that will overshadow our temporary pain, our Scriptures imply, we would never complain, not ever. We are given a promise: God's purposes for himself and for us make every ounce of suffering completely worthwhile for the redeemed.

There's a Connection

Nearly everyone used mightily by God in Scripture suffered. If we read some of the prayers of the sufferers, we notice that, for the most part, they were concerned not primarily with their own comfort but with the glory of God.

Moses is a prime example. After being disciplined by God on the backside of a desert for forty years, Moses was called to go to a dangerous pharaoh and make a dangerous demand:

let God's people go. All along the way, the people of God complained. In Egypt, they blamed Moses for making their brick production harder. At the edge of the Red Sea, they blamed Moses for leading them on a suicide mission. Across the Red Sea, they blamed Moses for leading them to places without water and food. Never mind that God provided and delivered every step of the way; there was suffering involved, and they were sure it wouldn't have happened if Moses hadn't butted in. It was his fault, they said over and over again. And when the complaining people got tired of waiting for Moses to come down from the mountain where God was, they built an idol and danced.

God made Moses an amazing offer in Exodus 32:10. He said he would destroy the chosen people and make a new nation out of Moses. Someone who had been accused by those people so pointedly could easily be forgiven for thinking about the proposal, but Moses didn't hesitate. Such wrath would undermine the promises of God, and the surrounding nations would not see God's glory, Moses argued. And God relented, averting the impending disaster.

A God of omniscience never doubted this outcome, of course. But we see in Moses's prayer a willingness to continue in difficulty for the benefit of glorifying God. His priority was not to get comfortable and free himself from the people who plagued him. It was to walk back into the fickle crowd so that other nations would see God for who he is.

We have seen how David, whose psalms revolve around the glory of God, suffered enormously. But we also see how his suffering was well tolerated for the sake of God's character. He went out into battle against a rabid giant because Goliath was slandering God. He refused to rid himself of a vengeful Saul, even with ample opportunity to do so, because killing the anointed king would defame God. He repented of his own sin, saying, "Against you, you only, have I sinned" (Ps. 51:4). His greatest ambition was to build a temple that would honor God. And his constant theme was well expressed in Psalm 27: "One thing have I asked of the LORD, . . . that I may dwell in the house of the LORD all the days of my life, to gaze upon the beauty of the LORD and to inquire in his temple" (v. 4). David wanted God's glory above all. Not his own comfort, not his own justification, not relief from his suffering. Glory first.

The greatest example, of course, is Jesus. It's no surprise that, centuries before the incarnation, the Incarnate One was described as a suffering servant in Isaiah's prophecies. The one who came to reveal God also came, not just coincidentally, to die a painful death. Jesus spoke often of the glory of God, and he spoke most often of God's glory the night before he was crucified. Yes, he knew the pain was coming. Yes, he wished he could have been delivered from it. But when it came down to a decision, Jesus opted for his own pain and the glory of God.

That's the choice we are often faced with: either our comfort at the expense of God's glory or God's glory at the expense of our comfort. As much as we would like to have both—God's glory and our comfort—that's rarely an option. It's one or the other. In the Bible, the godly examples always end up suffering so that God might reveal himself to them, in them, and through them. We don't like that choice, but it's unavoidable.

The connection between God's glory and our pain is constantly expressed in Scripture. Jesus told his followers they would have to count the cost of following him in a rebellious world. If they wanted to display his character within them, to have his Spirit living within them, they would have tribulation. The way of the cross is never comfortable, but it reveals God. It is the primary way for us to participate in his glory.

It may be hard to notice the utter God-centeredness of the Bible when we read it with human-centered eyes, but the true focus is indisputable. It's all about him—including our suffering. We, in our pain, are in a remarkable position for God to demonstrate his attributes that no heavenly creature had ever seen. He can reveal the beauty of his character in our desperate need, and he will if we let him.

A Legacy of Suffering

Long before the exodus, the patriarch who led the chosen family into Egypt in the first place got a glimpse of how God uses suffering for his glory and our own good. Joseph went through horrible trials—once in his brothers' rejection and once in an Egyptian dungeon. His brothers, after all, sold him to some wandering traders and returned home to tell his father that the beloved son was dead. As a slave in Egypt, he was the victim of a wicked lie. His master's wife tried to seduce him, and when he refused, he was falsely accused of sexual assault. It was either death or the dungeon. He might have preferred the former.

But when God raised Joseph up into a position of prestige second to only one—higher than all but Pharaoh himself—he had an appropriate perspective on his suffering. His children (through a prestigious priest's daughter) were given extremely significant names: Manasseh and Ephraim. The meaning of the first name spoke of the temporary nature of suffering: "one who causes to forget." God made Joseph forget all his troubles by blessing him extravagantly. The meaning of the second name was even more profound: "twice fruitful." God had made him doubly fruitful in the land of his affliction.

It was a kind of fruitfulness he could not have had back in Canaan, where life was good.

I doubt that Joseph looked ahead to the blessing of God either in the holding pit his brothers had thrown him into or in the dungeon Potiphar had thrown him into. He was patient and undoubtedly never lost faith in the goodness of God, but he surely had lots of questions. He probably struggled, wondering why his brothers had treated him with such vengeance, wondering why his obedience to God's moral standards had resulted in such shame, wondering why Pharaoh's cupbearer had forgotten for two years to tell the authorities about his good deeds, wondering why . . . well, just why. That's the same question we ask all throughout our lives whenever we suffer, and Joseph surely asked it too.

The important thing is to get to the place where Joseph ended up—blessed beyond his pain. And it really helps to see ahead to that blessing—to hang on to the promise of pain—when we're in the midst of suffering. Faith always results in such blessing. Always.

We can focus on the problem of pain and never come to any satisfactory answers. People have tried for millennia to sort that problem out. Instead of focusing on the problem of pain, God calls us to focus on the promise of pain. And, in God's revelation, that's a very concrete promise. It doesn't have any of the mystery the problem has, and it's more important.

Focusing on the promise won't lead us to accuse God of injustice or to deny the coexistence of his goodness, power, wisdom, and love. Focusing on the promise will accomplish exactly what the Bible encourages us to accomplish, like seeing the once invisible attributes of God with faith and looking ahead to the future glory of eternal blessing.

9

In the Eyes of Angels

I heard around the throne and the living creatures and the elders the voice of many angels, numbering myriads of myriads and thousands of thousands, saying with a loud voice, "Worthy is the Lamb who was slain, to receive power and wealth and wisdom and might and honor and glory and blessing!"

Revelation 5:11–12

Near one of the oldest towns in Bulgaria sits a rather typically nondescript monastery. It gets its share of tourists, primarily because it is of historical interest and parts of it lie in ruins. For that it is interesting, but only mildly, in the eyes of most visitors. Nevertheless, on select evenings throughout the year, a crowd gathers on one of the city's street corners with every eye fixed on the top of the hill where the monastery sits. Why? Because a spectacular laser show will light up the walls of the monastery in brilliant colors while dramatic music and narrative provide a compelling background. Ancient bricks and mortar known for centuries for their solid service to the Orthodox faithful are seen in a different light—literally—and architectural features that were not noticed in the daytime are suddenly and powerfully apparent. The audience, having nodded in admiration in the afternoon, will ooh and aah in amazement now. But they had to wait for one event before seeing the monastery in this light: the sky first had to become dark.

"Even angels long to look into these things." That's what Peter told a suffering church (1 Pet. 1:12 NIV). In the midst of their pain, he wrote of "a living hope," "an inheritance that is imperishable," "a salvation ready to be revealed," a faith more valuable than gold that will "result in praise and glory and honor at the revelation of Jesus Christ," and a joy that is "inexpressible and filled with glory" (1 Pet. 1:3–9).

These are not phrases we generally use when we ache. But Peter spoke them without fear of sounding pious or superficial. They were not pat answers, yet they were still overwhelmingly positive. This whole salvation plan, the end of this entire painful earth experience, is summed up in "the sufferings of Christ and the subsequent glories," he says (v. 11). The prophets looked ahead to it, the Spirit of Christ spoke of it, and the early apostles preached it. It's the common thread of the New Testament. Death is swallowed up in victory (1 Corinthians 15), all creation groans for its redemption (Romans 8), a heavenly kingdom is being built, and suffering precedes glory. "Even angels long to look into these things."

That's the drama of it all. There's an audience. This whole earth expedition—the Garden of Eden, the fall of humankind, the revelation of the law, the failure of our sinful race to keep it, the sacrifice of the God-man for our redemption, the advent of the Holy Spirit in the hearts of human beings, the ministry of the body of Christ, and the day of final judgment and the revelation of Jesus Christ in all his glory—is being played out in front of an enormous crowd. Our fallen planet is the night that provides the background to the show. Everything that has gone into this strange, amazing work of the Creator's hand is there to be seen. Angels are oohing and aahing over it now, as the darkness has fallen and the light has begun to shine. All of the created beings we have speculated about, those creatures who did not—who could not—see the mercies of the almighty, holy, powerful, eternal God now know the definition of compassion, grace, forgiveness, restoration, deliverance, healing, and love that knows no conditions. They have witnessed it. It is not just a declaration God gave to Moses when he revealed himself on the mountain. It is not just the words of Scripture—potent but obscure. There is a living illustration of it in God's plan of salvation. The scars of Jesus are eternal. The story of God's mercies is a living, everlasting testimony.

But, as we have noted repeatedly, none of it would have happened unless we—or some creation somewhere—suffered.

Hidden Witnesses

Speculating about angels is a risky endeavor. They are a part of the unseen world that will become much clearer to us one day when we are no longer so emphatically physical. We have heard stories about the rebellion in heaven. Lucifer, we are told, was given a high position but wanted a higher one, and he was aggressive about it. But there is only one ultimate throne, and it belongs to God. There wasn't room in heaven for two sovereigns. Lucifer had to go, and Jesus watched his demise. "I saw Satan fall like lightning from heaven," he told his disciples (Luke 10:18).

Who was this sick creature? The archangel Michael seems to be a warrior (see Dan. 10:13; 12:1; Jude 9), and the archangel Gabriel seems to be a messenger (see Dan. 9:22; Luke 1:26–38). Was Lucifer an archangel of worship—the leading archangel of worship—as Ezekiel 28:13–14 may imply? Did he sing songs of praise before he yearned to be the object of them? He seems to have his hand in a lot of music now; is he perverting his background as a once sacred artist? Did his familiarity with God's glory breed the contempt he now has for it? What weakness did he think he saw in the most high God that made him believe he could occupy that position? Did he mistake God's humility for vulnerability? What could he possibly have experienced in heaven that would inspire such lunacy? Perhaps we'll never know the answers to these questions. Or perhaps one day we will. For now, Scripture gives us only hints.

There are some things we can know for sure: Satan hates God. His agenda makes that clear. He also seems to hate the fact that God can take such weak, ignoble, sin-struck creatures as ourselves and make us one with Christ, bringing us into blissful, worshipful fellowship with the Trinity. That's where he wanted to be! He thought his high position qualified him. How could humans of such low position possibly be qualified? What an unexpected replacement we are. It must grate on him with undying annoyance.

We have learned something Lucifer forgot: we can only fulfill the purpose for which God created us. Lucifer was made to praise God's image. We were made in it. We were given the higher position he craved, and the void of praise his exit left behind is to be filled with us. And, honestly, don't fallen creatures restored to God's image reflect his greatness and sacrifice much better than an unfallen being of the highest order? Of course we do. Satan apparently hates that.

So how does this relate to our pain? What is the promise of pain in this obscure picture of the fallen one?

Consider this: Lucifer apparently thought there was glory in self-exaltation. Perhaps our world is the cosmic object lesson that there is glory in suffering. The character of God cannot be usurped by anyone, much less a creature who knows only a part of it. Did Lucifer know about mercy and compassion and deliverance and redemption when he swelled up with pride? If we go back to our speculation about the choruses of praise before the foundation of our world, we would have to ask, "On what basis? How would he have known? Who *could* have known?"

Mercy once was invisible. In the absence of a fall, in the perfect milieu of heaven, in the hours or eons when brokenness was a foreign concept, no one could have seen this side of God. Lucifer likely wouldn't have even been interested in the throne had he known there is a side of God that would suffer with his hurting loved ones and that there are aspects of God's character that would drive him toward a costly redemption. The earth experience is the ultimate illustration: there is much about God that neither Lucifer nor any other created being had ever considered.

The fall of Lucifer and his fellow rebels may have led to such questions among angelic hosts: Is there any way to win them back? Is it possible to be restored after such an offensive mutiny? Can this rift in heaven be reconciled in the character of the Holy? While mercy is not applied to Satan or his followers, as the Bible makes clear,[1] it is nevertheless the essential core of the Godhead. Maybe this world is the evidence. Maybe it is the divine demonstration that answers all the questions asked in the aftermath of the angelic treason. Maybe the revelation of God's mercy is as astonishing in heaven as the revelation of a fourth dimension on earth would be to our narrow minds. Maybe the worshiping archangel will be forced to acknowledge in his condemnation that he never quite knew whom he was worshiping. Maybe we in our suffering are displaying things about God that all of existence will forever be able to praise.

Just maybe.

Depending on the Promise

I mentioned earlier that my son was in a car accident and is now living with a severe brain injury. It was only a month after he got his driver's license, and though he was not doing anything illegal or reckless, he was clearly demonstrating his inexperience. Looking back, it's easy to wonder, What if . . . ? What if he had been on that road two seconds earlier or two seconds later? What if he had seen the other driver signal? What if he had taken an alternate route home or stopped for a snack at the drive-through? What if his curfew had been a half hour earlier or later? What if I had done a better job of training him to drive? Any number of slight changes in history—in the schedule or the conditions or his mentality—could have averted that dreadful accident. Instead, it happened. A helicopter flew him to a hospital fifty miles away, he lay in a coma for six weeks, and our lives changed. Especially his.

There are certain struggles a person goes through when confronted with tragedy, and almost all of them are valid. There's no shame in wondering why God let it happen, or even if he wasn't powerful enough to prevent it. There's nothing inherently evil in wondering if this tragedy was the result of sin or just some divine cruelty. There is a problem, however, with cultivating and embracing those misunderstandings. God has given us a better angle on the whole mess; it's up to us to choose it.

Most of my family members have done so, though not without temptations otherwise. I realized I had a choice. I could question the reality of God's revelation—which certainly does not hide the fact of evil and suffering—or I could embrace the hope that God clearly gives us in his revelation. I chose the latter.

God's truth never encourages us to ask "what if" ad nauseam until we've driven ourselves crazy. It never even hints that God might have been less than good or less than powerful in our situation. What it does is provide us with a solid basis for hope. It tells us that the fallenness of our world is a temporary condition, and if we look at circumstances from within it, we may despair, but if we look at circumstances from the viewpoint of eternity, we can count on the sovereignty of God to make it all worthwhile.

For me, it's comforting to think that God is now showing himself and will continue to show himself in my son's tragedy. Though right now Christopher has severe physical problems (he's blind in one eye, walks off balance, and has obvious nervous system impairments) and also severe behavioral problems (he is injured in the part of the brain that governs social interactions and controls rash impulses), any or all of that could change. Maybe after demonstrating what a human being without any impulse control is like, God will give Christopher self-control by the power of his Spirit. Maybe God will use this long-term crisis to demonstrate the faith of family members, or the patience of those who suffer with Christopher, or the miracle of one young man's perseverance in the face of hardship, or even the drama of a complete, miraculous healing.

We don't know what God is doing in the situation right now. We may not know that for years. But we do know one thing: the situation is a platform for God to show himself.

He can show himself strong, comforting, powerful, compassionate, methodical, miraculous, or all of the above. He has the suffering of a teenager and the anguish of a family to pour himself into, and he will. There are attributes of our Creator that we never would have experienced if our tragedy had not happened. God is revealing himself, and he will continue to do so.

How and when? We'll see—one day, at least, if not soon. It's a promise.

PART 3

THE PROBLEMS

Will what is molded say to its molder, "Why have you made me like this?"

Romans 9:20

10

Eternity in Their Eyes

We know that for those who love God all things work together for good, for those who are called according to his purpose.

Romans 8:28

She was a young mother of two beautiful children. She was a faithful, Christ-honoring believer who served her church, her family, and her community well. When news of her cancer broke, hundreds of people began praying. We prayed zealously and persistently, lifting her up to our Father in faith and trust, claiming his promises and relying on his character. Within a year she was dead.

That's a common story, isn't it? It isn't always the story—we're familiar with God's powerful works, because we've seen them from time to time. But often we don't, and that's frustrating. We serve a God who not only promises to meet us in our suffering but also gives us numerous examples of his deliverance from that suffering. Our Scripture is filled not only with pain upon pain but also with miracle upon miracle. It gets our hopes up. And then, quite frequently, the God who is known for pouring his mercy into a hurting world seems to withhold it. Why?

This question is the essence of Gideon's lament in Judges 6: "If the LORD is with us, why then has all this happened to us? And where are all his wonderful deeds that our fathers recounted to us?" (v. 13). The answer is what every disease-ridden person and every grief-afflicted soul does not want to hear: sometimes the glory is displayed in ways other than an immediate miracle.

When you're desperate for a miracle, that's not the answer you want. You want a promise of deliverance, of healing, of some clear, unambiguous evidence of mercy. God is full of promises, and we may take him at his word. But he is often more subtle than we'd like. Sometimes he has other purposes for our pain.

The early Christians certainly knew of Daniel's deliverance from the lions' den. They had heard of God's miraculous power not only through such Old Testament stories but also within their own communities. Peter had been delivered from prison, and so had Paul and Barnabas. If tradition is correct, those early believers had also heard how John was put into a boiling cauldron of oil, only to come out unscathed—echoes of the fiery furnace of Babylon and the God who is able to save. Not only had the God of miracles worked powerfully in the past, he was working among them.

But God didn't always shut the mouths of lions for these believers. Some of them were devoured in the arenas. Though Peter was delivered from prison, James and Stephen were killed. Though Paul was given many escapes, he was also given many beatings and incarcerations. The God who let Jesus die on the cross was letting many of his followers walk the same path. Wouldn't his glory have been well displayed with miraculously passive lions and constantly breaking chains? Maybe so, but it was also well displayed in the suffering. The blood-hungry crowds saw eternity in the eyes of dying believers, just as the promising young lawyer named Saul saw it in Stephen when he was being stoned. The church was built on the blood of the martyrs; Scripture and tradition are clear about that. The fact that there were eternal realities greater than the agenda of the emperor made a profound impression on observers. God grew his church through dying witnesses.

Romanus was a fourth-century believer who was martyred in Antioch. When told he would be burned, he maintained a cheerful expression. When his tongue was cut out, he bore the pain with great courage and strength. He died nobly, witnessing without a word to the fact that eternal life could not be taken from him. Eusebius, bishop of Caesarea and the early church historian who tells us of Romanus, wrote that "he proved his actions to all, showing also that the power of God is always present to the aid of those who are obliged to bear any hardship for the sake of religion, to lighten their labors and strengthen their ardor." Sociologist Rodney Stark notes that Eusebius saw the bravery of the martyrs as proof of Christian virtues, and "indeed, many pagans were deeply impressed."[1] We may want to ask why God would not have been glorified with a miraculous deliverance of Romanus from his pagan oppressors, but the hindsight of history shows us a greater glory. We see deeper values and a spirit of eternity at work in the lives of those who suffer.

That's frequently the way of God, isn't it? We must not rule out the possibility of incredible miracles that display his power. They have happened throughout Scripture, throughout history, and throughout our world today. We've heard the testimonies and often seen the evidence ourselves. But miracles aren't always the answer. Sometimes the glory of God is seen in the calm of the sufferer. Sometimes it is seen in the endurance of the tormented. Sometimes the power of God is made manifest through the frailties of the sick or the crippled or the apostle with a thorn in his flesh (2 Corinthians 12). We'd love to see the miracle, but sometimes we are to *be* the miracle. When we suffer, others must see eternity in our eyes.

Over and over again, in Christian circles, we hear testimonies of people with some sort of infirmity or handicap who say they have learned so much more about God in their pain than they would have otherwise. In fact, many, if given the opportunity to change their past adverse circumstances, would opt not to do so. There's a common refrain among infirm Christians, summed up well by the sick mother of a friend: "I would rather be sick and know what I've learned about God than be healthy and not know what I've learned." That's one reason our prayers are often unanswered, and it supports the core message of this book: in the context of suffering, the compassionate side of God comes through.

Does It Have to Be This Bad?

There are larger questions than our personal suffering though. What about the Holocaust? What about the killing fields? Nazi Germany and Cambodia, as well as Rwanda, Bosnia, Sudan, North Korea, and anywhere else we've seen widespread death, destruction, famine, and plague, are our biggest obstacles to accepting the glory of God as an excuse for an evil world. We can hardly imagine the purpose in such devastation. The physical pain, the emotional scars, the psychological wounds, the spiritual cancers that characterize such places are staggering. Horrible. Cataclysmic. Our words fail us.

How, in God's name, can that agony be justified? What kind of God would let that sort of crisis happen in order to set a stage for his own purposes? Ours, apparently. If we believe in the sovereignty of God, we have to believe he lets those things happen. We don't blame him for them, of course; that wouldn't be theologically sophisticated—or accurate. But we know that he knows about them, and that he could intervene, and that he doesn't. And the question continues to nag us. Why?

I don't know. I do know that these abhorrent events are integral to a fallen world and that this fallen world is ravaged by the evil one. I also know that this present suffering is temporary and that, in the eternal perspective, it will seem like a blip on the screen or a point in the time line; it is excruciating, but the horrific pain will end and appear very limited in scope. From our perspective, it is utterly devastating, but we freely admit that we have a very limited perspective. We are bound by space and time, and we can hardly imagine an eternity with no beginning and no end. And in addition to the vengeance of the evil one and the temporary nature of our broken world, I also know that God has made us that promise we've discussed: in the end, all the glory will outweigh all the pain.

We don't know exactly why the Holocaust and the killing fields and all the other horrors happened, but we know some things about God from Scripture. He is both merciful and righteous, and to us that's a strange mix. It's a mystery to us how God's mercy and human treachery can be wrapped up in the same bundle, but they often are. And then there's the problem of judgment. In a blatantly mutinous world, we must leave room for the wrath of God, even when we don't understand it. In the Old Testament, God harshly judged the entire world with a flood, saving only Noah's family, and the text clearly asserts that God was justified in his harshness. Later God used pagan Babylonians to discipline his treasured people of Judah, who, according to the prophets, deserved it; then he turned around and judged the Babylonians, who also deserved it. These harsh realities are aspects of a planet in rebellion, and God is fully able to protect us from the effects of rebellion. Often he doesn't. That's his prerogative, and we can assume he has redemptive purposes—or at least just ones—in his decisions.

Sometimes the glory is in the aftermath. We've all heard of God's mercies in saving and restoring people during and after a tragedy. We more profoundly appreciate what is good and pure after being subjected to what is vile and disgusting. The healing after devastation can point to God.

Sometimes the glory is in the harvest. No seed flourishes in untilled soil, so the soil must be broken up. But that's a violent event. Though genocides and wars brutally till the soil, seeds often flourish afterward. Cambodia and Rwanda are now two of the most responsive places on the planet, not in spite of their past horrors, but because of them. Isaiah's prophecy is sadly true: "When your judgments are in the earth, the inhabitants of the world learn righteousness" (Isa. 26:9).

And sometimes the glory is in the church's response. We've all heard of people who have well represented the merciful character of God in the context of these events, just as God himself does. I have a hunch that when we behold a situation so bleak that we wonder where God's glory is, the answer is in the beholder. We're looking for a supernatural intervention, and God is waiting for an ecclesiastical intervention. We watch for the glory to be revealed, and he watches for it to be revealed in us. While we wonder what God's response is going to be, we forget to look in the mirror. We're God's response. His glory is displayed in his church, the body of Christ.

So why the disaster? It depends on the disaster. Sometimes the reason is for God's deliverance to be miraculously demonstrated. Sometimes it is for God's judgment and wrath on a society. Sometimes it is for prompting repentance in preparation for an outpouring of his grace. Sometimes it is for the perseverance and the patience of the believers in the disaster. Sometimes it is for the world to see eternity in the eyes of the sufferers. Sometimes it's all of the above—and more. *But there is always something.* In every circumstance, there is some glimpse of God's glory to behold, some aspect of his character to hang on to. Sometimes it may be his power, sometimes only his comfort, but there is always something, if we will look for it.

God takes no pleasure in evil; we can be sure of that. But we can also be sure he redeems it for his purposes. John Piper, referring to a thought from Puritan theologian Jonathan Edwards, says, "The infinite complexity of the divine mind is such that God has the capacity to look at the world through two lenses. He can look through a narrow lens or through a wide-angle lens. . . . When God looks at a painful or wicked event through his wide-angle lens, he sees the tragedy or the sin in relation to everything leading up to it and everything flowing out from it."[2] In other words, he sees it with eternity in view. We don't.

That's where the glory is. It is in eternity, in the long view, in the sheer weight of the blessings to be revealed when all is said and done. Add up all the aggregate pain of every holocaust, captivity, massacre, betrayal, flood, and famine, and it will not outweigh the glory of God that is now being revealed or the blessing to be shared with the redeemed. Just because we can't see that from Cambodia or Sudan doesn't mean it isn't true. The glory is always there, and one day we will see it more fully.

The Beauty of the Oasis

> Be merciful to me, LORD, for I am faint; O LORD, heal me, for my bones are in agony. My soul is in anguish. How long, O LORD, how long?
>
> Psalm 6:2–3 NIV

How well I remember hot summer days in the neighborhood when I was a boy. My friends and I would play the sport of choice—football, baseball, basketball, or maybe some odd competition of our own invention—until we were drenched with sweat on the outside and as dry as dust on the inside. I remember the burning sensation of extreme thirst and how pleasant even a sip of cool water from the garden hose was. I remember the baking sensation from the sun and how pleasant even a brief swim in the neighborhood pool was. The drinking water and the swimming pool were mildly enjoyable anytime, but they were thoroughly savored on Georgia's hundred-degree August afternoons.

We often wonder why there is such a long delay between our cries to God and his deliverance. If he is so merciful, why does he tarry? Why are there so many biblical commands to wait on the Lord? Does he lengthen our suffering for nothing? Our pain is urgent to us; why not to him?

We may never know all the reasons God delays the visible expressions of his mercies. Sometimes he shows up in a hurry, but often he does not. There are surely a multitude of possible reasons: his formation of our character, his work on other people involved in our situation, the ability to hold our attention longer when we're suffering than when we're free and easy, the development of our prayer habits. His delays have many purposes, and they aren't always about us.

But there is still something unsettling about the idea that we cry out to a merciful God and then wait. And wait. And wait. How does the delay fit with this idea that our broken world exists for him to demonstrate himself in all his compassion and grace? If that's why we suffer, we want to hurry and beg the outcome. We want him to go ahead and display himself.

I've often wondered if my appreciation for God's character is only as deep as my craving for its appearance. There's plenty of evidence in my own life to suggest that this is so. When I have a momentary craving, I often only give momentary thanks when the fulfillment comes. When I crave deeply—for years, even—and the answer finally comes, the victory party is great. I exuberantly, passionately worship and thank God for his intervention as surely as huge gulps follow a season in the desert. Perhaps deep worship should be evident even when the answers are immediate, but I know it will not be. The human heart is rarely so generous. It's a matter of context; we often don't grasp the wonderful aspects of life unless hardship highlights them for us. We have to nearly starve before we really become thankful for food. We have to first be anxious and scared before we begin to value security. An oasis is only appreciated when the barren wasteland surrounding it is vast. Otherwise, it's just a fertile area among other fertile areas.

The Power of Delay

There is plenty of biblical evidence that God's delays bring him greater glory. The Bible frequently uses childbirth to illustrate this. Abraham and Sarah waited for the son of promise. And they waited. The point of impossibility came and went. And then, after Sarah and apparently even Abraham had given up hope, after they had tried all their human means and failed, God showed up. He put his miracle where his promise had been. The son of promise was the son of laughter—an oddity beyond all oddities but a delightful one to say the least. Fertility appeared in the midst of decades of barrenness. The celebration was sweet.

We can say the same of Isaac and Rebekah just a few chapters later in Genesis. The son of laughter's wife was barren too. He prayed. She conceived. The celebration again was sweet. And in 1 Samuel Hannah endured much mockery and scorn from her rival because of her barrenness. When God finally gave her a son, Hannah gave us an eternally recorded song of praise that is overflowing in its gratitude. Out of the barrenness came fertility. Out of the fertility came praise. It would have been hardly noticed—perhaps a brief "Elkanah begat Samuel"—had the context not been futility.

Then the theme carries over to the New Testament. After four hundred years of a prophetless Israel between the Testaments, after decades of childlessness for Zechariah and Elizabeth, God spoke into the desert. Out of the barrenness, God brought John the Baptist, the prophet preparing the way for Jesus. The celebration continues today.

The examples are certainly not limited to women who were late in conceiving. What about Israel and its four hundred years of slavery in Egypt? Why not just a couple of decades of slavery? I don't know, but I'm guessing the celebration on the far side of the Red Sea would have been less than half as sweet if God had delivered a large family after a generation or two of captivity.

The Bible is full of examples of people just waiting and waiting and waiting, sinking deeper into silent resignation.

Then God shows up in a dramatic way. The bigger the deliverance, the greater the glory displayed. The longer the barrenness, the happier the birth. The deeper the pain, the more appreciated the comfort. The more extended the illness, the sweeter the healing. It's not a hard principle—unless we're in the middle of it.

If you are suffering, you want God to hurry. Maybe he will. He holds all timing in his hands, and though he works in our lives slowly and thoroughly, he will not let pain linger longer than it has to. He promises that he will deliver his people out of all their troubles (see, for example, Ps. 34:6, 17, 19; 107:19–20). He does not promise when, but he does promise that he will. His answer is enjoyable anytime, but it's thoroughly savored at the far side of a desert.

When mercy flows it will be as refreshing as a late summer rain, as soothing as a cool pool on a brutal August day in the South. "It will be said on that day, 'Behold, this is our God; we have waited for him, that he might save us. . . . Let us be glad and rejoice in his salvation" (Isa. 25:9). We may take a long time to get to the oasis, but the longer we take, the sweeter it will be. The length of the wait and the depth of the thirst will result in a corresponding increase in praise and glory for the one who provides it. And that's really what it's all about.

11

What Kind of Love?

The one who seeks the glory of him who sent him is true, and in him there is no falsehood.

John 7:18

The grove was ordinarily empty this time of night, but this was no ordinary night. A few men lay still on the ground or propped up against tree trunks. They were drifting in and out of sleep. Several yards beyond them, however, one figure writhed in emotional agony. Sweat mixed with blood as he poured out his anguish in prayer. He was talking to an unseen Father, begging for a plan B that would take away the pain that was to come. But in the end he submitted to the pain. Why? Because of a prayer he had just prayed minutes before.

That prayer is preoccupied with glory. Jesus's prayer for his disciples in John 17 is almost obsessed with the idea. Nine times in this brief chapter the words *glory* or *glorify* are used.

And the context for such glory is the incarnation: "that they know you the only true God, and Jesus Christ whom you have sent" (v. 3). And the prayer closes with the same emphasis: "I made known to them your name, and I will continue to make it known" (v. 26). On the brink of pouring out his life for love, Jesus prays almost exclusively about the glory of God and the revelation of God's nature.

Jesus sought God's glory above all. That ultimate priority showed up in his teaching, as the words at the beginning of this chapter, as well as his actions, indicate. Did it lead to pain? We know it did. But there was a higher purpose. Suffering was part of the process that showed us what God is like. He even knew that ahead of time: "Father, the hour has come; glorify your Son that the Son may glorify you" (John 17:1). The demonstration of the Father and the Son would be an agonizing event, but the glory would be greater.

That's our example. We cannot complain about our suffering to a God who knows suffering more intimately than we do.

Our concept of God, particularly in recent Western culture, has been based primarily on love as his foremost characteristic. Suffering clashes with that concept. It doesn't contradict his love as it really is; it contradicts his love as we have come to define it. Somehow we got the impression that the love of God means he should not tolerate our suffering. Our idea of love involves comfort and esteem building. God's love includes heavy doses of character building and a radical redirection of our affections from ourselves to him. He wants us to be strong and love him with all our hearts. That means his honor will become our holy preoccupation.

This hasn't always been a foreign concept. In centuries past there seemed to be no conflict in the minds of parents between love for their children and resolve to discipline them.

In fact, these two concerns did not compete; they went hand in hand. We rarely see that combination anymore. Our society has defined love as acquiescence and affection. Our parenting reflects that. We have little room in our love for allowing suffering or deprivation. As a result, we have a hard time reconciling our understanding of God—who is love—with the suffering we see in the world. Our love would rule it out. But biblical love is not so defined.

Part of the problem we have in reconciling God's love and suffering is the intensity of the suffering we see. Excruciating pain is more drastic than grounding our child who came in late. The trials we go through are often far from trivial. They are devastating.

As indicated earlier, the real problem is our human-centered point of view. We think the world revolves around us. God's love is an emphatic biblical principle, but we misinterpret it as his placing us in the divine center, such that everything that happens is either for the welfare or for the detriment of human beings. We see the cross as being not for God's purposes but for ours. When we see God incarnate dying on behalf of sinful humanity, we think perhaps that it ends there, that this is the whole point. But not only is he doing something for our benefit out of his great love, but he has an even more ultimate purpose in mind. He is doing something for his own benefit that will more greatly reflect his own glory.[1]

We see God's love as his guiding principle, but his love has another guiding principle: it supports and treasures his glory. This is clear in numerous scriptural texts, Isaiah 48 being a prime example. God actively put his people in a painful situation to discipline them, and he makes the reason abundantly clear: "I have tried you in the furnace of affliction. *For my own sake, for my own sake,* I do it, for how should my name be profaned? My glory I will not give to another" (Isa. 48:10–11). In other words, his glory was more important than Israel's comfort. God's loving agenda includes an audience that can praise his worth—even if there is a heavy, heavy cost. The chosen people's pain was for his sake.

Here's an illustration. Your love for your mate can feel deep and intense, but if it revolves around making your wife or husband always feel good, then it is really a shallow kind of love. What other principles should guide it? The emotional health of the couple, the long-term interests of the relationship, compatibility on issues such as finances or parenting, a shared ministry, and so forth. In all of these areas, comfort and pleasure may take a backseat to the more ultimate goal. Love and gratification do not always sit well together. To use a phrase from counseling circles, sometimes love must be tough. Hard issues and love are not mutually exclusive.

In the same way, God's love does not imply that we won't have hard issues. We may wonder why he doesn't seem to meet our deep needs immediately and mend our broken hearts or broken bodies. But that's just our tendency to think it's all about us. It rarely occurs to us, but maybe we should consider more often what purpose God might have in our difficulties.

Some might argue that the quest to find glory in suffering—a quest in which God wins regardless of the situation—is a hopeful human's tendency to rationalize the existence and goodness of God. Perhaps so, but there's no denying that many people have experienced awful things and learned a lot from their difficulties. God is findable both in the miracle and in the absence thereof. Either way, there can always be something in our suffering for him as well as for us.

We would do well to ask hard questions about God's agenda—not "Why, for my purposes, am I going through this?" but "Why, for your purposes, am I going through this?" Are we mature enough to ask that? Can we get to the point where we see ourselves as his instruments even in pain? Are we aware that human affairs are not always completely about humans, that sometimes our suffering can be a sacrifice of genuine worship? If we remember that our need is often there to reveal something about God to a God-hungry world—and also to a heavenly host that is curious about this whole mercy business—that's exactly what our pain becomes: worship.

An Offering of Pain

Once we get it deeply embedded in our minds that our suffering can be a platform for the display of God, we can begin to rely on its larger purpose. Every leper and every blind, possessed, hurting person who ever came to Jesus became such a platform. Their pain led to a demonstration of his glory, and so can ours. We begin to see ourselves in that position. We hope, of course, for his glory to be dramatically displayed in us. But even if it is not, we know the display can be there in much more subtle ways, or that it will be there in dramatic ways at the end of the act.

The blind man in John 9—you remember, the one whose blindness was not from sin but "that the works of God might be displayed in him" (v. 3)—became a whole act of John's drama. Tossed about by the theological nuances of the culture and the personal agendas of the Pharisees, the man finally threw his hands up and declared, "Listen, you folks can argue about this guy all you want; all I know is I was blind and now I see!" (John 9:25, my paraphrase).

In a sense, this should become our attitude toward all of our pain. It is no longer about us. It's about God and what he can do. Essentially, we have two appropriate responses to our suffering: we should expect God's once invisible character to be demonstrated to us—somehow, some way, in his own time—and we should reflect his once invisible character for others to see. Both responses glorify him. Our hurts become for us an offering—our offering of pain.

Let me clarify what I mean by this kind of sacrifice. Any sacrifice can be painful; our genuine offerings to God should cost us dearly in terms of resources or effort. But I'm not talking just about giving offerings that cost us something. There will come a time in our suffering when the pain itself becomes our offering to God. We cease our inward focus on the intensity of our trial and ask God to use it for himself. Usually it is the moment when we are completely overwhelmed, when all we know to do is to curl up in the fetal position, suck our thumb, and wish it would all be over soon. When you find yourself in that position, literally or figuratively, instead of asking God why this is happening to you, ask him what he wants to do with it. Turn your pain around toward him and offer it up as a sacrifice of service. Tell him that if he can find it useful, then it will be worthwhile. He may make a miracle of it. He may not. But he will do something with it, and it will be good.

What about Job?

> You have heard of the steadfastness of Job, and you have seen the purpose of the Lord, how the Lord is compassionate and merciful.
>
> James 5:11

No one knows exactly what to do with Job. We marvel at his patience and consistent faith, but in the end we throw our hands up and say it's a lesson in enduring even when we don't know what God is up to. When God finally speaks to Job, he defends his right to divine mysteries and unknowable sovereignty. But we can't go much further than that. Even expert commentaries are frequently vague. All we know from Job is that there are times when we just can't know.

I've heard Bible teachers say that the main lesson of Job is that God does not put a hedge around his people. (The text clearly illustrates that he does and that the removal of it in Job's case is an exception.) Some teachers attribute all of Job's woes to Satan. (Isn't it God who first offers Job as a test case for authentic worship?) Some teachers assert that in the book of Job, even God wrestles with evil. (Doesn't the book end with God—the *creator* of Leviathan, Behemoth, and every other big, bad physical or spiritual creature—defending his wisdom and sovereignty?) There are abundant analyses of Job, and many of them are off base. I think part of the reason for that is that no one wants to face up to the obvious: God used Job as a human pawn in a spiritual showdown.

I hesitate to use the word *pawn*, because that implies something trivial, and we are emphatically *not* trivial in God's eyes. His love never trivializes his creation. If he knows when a sparrow falls, as Jesus assures us, he certainly values his people. What I mean by being a pawn of God is certainly not that he carelessly uses us for selfish purposes. He is not a utilitarian consumer of precious things, which people made in his image clearly are. What I mean is that God integrated Job's suffering into his overarching strategy. He sacrificed Job's comfort for the higher purpose of making his own glory known. We shouldn't be surprised if he does that with us as well.

Our instincts want to offer a disclaimer that vindicates God: that he allowed our suffering but didn't plan it. But, in Job's case, he did more than allow it. He *ordained* it, even initiated the conversation about it before it happened.

Satan is guilty of it, but God is more than a passive observer. He is sovereign over the process. In foreknowledge, he brought up Job as a case study. That makes Job—and us—feel like pawns, and we find that we have to remind ourselves frequently that God is a generous, loving rewarder of those precious lives that have been used to further his revelation of glory.

Still, in spite of the precious and priceless manner in which we were created—in the image of almighty God, no less—the book of Job seems to portray us as tokens. Is that too blunt? Doesn't that statement—and the rest of this book, for that matter—accuse God, despite my disclaimers to the contrary, of using us for utilitarian purposes? Doesn't that make him out to be callous and unloving? On the surface, yes. But let's dig a little deeper. Instead of crafting a God of our own imagination and desire, let's look at the God who is actually in the text.

Have you considered Job? Here's a guy who was our idea of a good person, if ever there was one. Contrary to his typical pattern in the Bible, especially the Old Testament, God does not reward good for good and bad for bad in Job's case. Job's goodness results in his being used as a test case. God's glory in his creation is at stake—the adversary questions the authenticity of human worship of the divine. According to his nature, Satan has been looking for someone to accuse, and God—not Satan—comes up with the idea of considering Job as a prime example of true worship. Satan charges that the deck is stacked in Job's favor.

So God turns the pawn over to the enemy. It's a challenge. A bet. Lives are at stake; a human being will, along with his family, languish and scream in pain; and his friends will stretch their brains to come up with the reason behind it all—just like we do. All because of a bet between God and his enemy.

Is God . . . Selfish?

"That's not fair!" our human instincts want to cry out. Why is that our impulse? Because we are far more concerned with our welfare than with the glory of God, to put it bluntly. We're much more interested in a God of love whose entire being revolves around our welfare, comfort, and plans. While God has amazingly, inexplicably lavished his love on us, that is not all he is about. Yes, 1 John 4:8 says, "God is love," but that doesn't mean that we're the only object of his love and that his love is governed by no other purpose than looking out for our concerns. There is so much more at stake in this creation than our welfare. The God who made it is its ultimate value, his glory the ultimate good. *Everything* is governed by that.

So while we're consumed with questions of why God did not seem to love Job properly—and, by implication, why he does not love us properly when we suffer—God is consumed with his own honor, reputation, fame, splendor, and majesty. In other words, his glory.

We are compelled to ask, "If God let this world fall in order to prove something about his own character, isn't he selfish?" He clearly used that dynamic with Job, letting his servant suffer to show something about himself. The first and easiest answer is that God makes our pain so worthwhile that it is actually a benefit to us, not a sacrifice. Many biblical writers make that clear; see Romans 8:18; 2 Corinthians 4:17; James 1:2; and 1 Peter 1:3–9, for example. All of those verses affirm that joy in the midst of persecution and suffering is possible; more than that, it's thoroughly integral to the teachings of Jesus and all the New Testament writers, as well as the Old Testament prophets and psalmists. Would I be selfish if I made my son eat his least favorite vegetable now so he could have his favorite dessert later? Not in the least. Neither is God.

But we're not talking about vegetables, are we? We're talking about disaster and death. So how can we reconcile this God who seeks his own glory even through our suffering, this God who is into revealing himself and asking for our worship, this God who selflessly clothed himself in human flesh, washed the dirty feet of sinful disciples, and bled and died for our salvation? On the one hand, he seems selfish. On the other, he clearly isn't.

It's a confusing proposition to those of us who are comfortable with a God of love and not a God of infinite intrinsic worth. Yes, he sacrificed his own Son for our salvation. But I would suggest that, while he loves us greatly, he might not have made that sacrifice unless it simultaneously revealed something of his magnificent mercy. His love for us who have fallen and his love for truth pull against one another. His love for truth means that he values what is truly valuable; he does not let himself be guided by that which is ultimately unworthy. As we have emphasized, the highest value in this universe is him. That is his guiding principle. And yet, because part of his glorious character is love and mercy, he simply *must* save those who have fallen.

Of course, there is really no conflict within the character of God. That's why we have the cross. Those two competing loves meet at the scene of the sacrifice. His love for his own glory—this ultimately valuable commodity—and his love for his fallen creatures are reconciled in a bloody God-man on a hill in Jerusalem. They are mysteriously interwoven in the incarnation. The death of Jesus perfectly demonstrates both the love of glory and the love of sinful humanity. In Jesus's death, mercy is complete. It demonstrates who God is, thereby glorifying him, and it demonstrates his selflessness.

It cost him a lot to do that. That adds to the glory, because it better illustrates the selflessness. It adds to the selflessness, because there was such glory from which to stoop.

The answer to the question of whether God is selfish is no. He is self-centered, not in an arrogant human sense, but in the sense that all things in this universe, God included, are appropriately either centered around God or classified as sinful and rebellious. God-centeredness reflects truth and ultimate value. It's right for everyone, including God.[2] But he is not selfish. He places ultimate value on his own glory, but he has found a way for that guiding value not to interfere with his selfless love. They complement one another. In mercy, in forgiveness—in Jesus—glory and humility meet.

Job would have no problem with that. He now knows the rest of the story as he sits in heaven and looks back. Do you think he wonders whether the sacred bet was worth it? He would scoff at the question. God rewards his pawns highly; he turns them into trophies and crowns them with honor. Their pain is not for nothing. There is glory in it—his and theirs. That's what James acknowledges in his inspired retrospective: "You have heard of the steadfastness of Job, and you have seen the purpose of the Lord, how the Lord is compassionate and merciful" (5:11). The pain of a pawn of God illustrates God's incredible mercy and selflessness. It also points to glory. God knows the process firsthand, because he clothed himself in humanity and became one of his own pawns.

Strikingly, the book of Job can be read as an illustration of the entire human condition. Like Job, we start out blessed. Somewhere early on we experience the decay of human corruption. God uses us in all our frailties as evidence of his glory, making us the stage for his mercies, and it puts us in an exceedingly painful position. Like Job and his friends, we struggle to understand that. But if we maintain our integrity in faith, then things are worthwhile—doubly better than we could have hoped[3]—in the end. We've got no business accepting as biblical this dynamic of Job's life while rejecting it as an explanation of evil and suffering on a grand scale.

The story of Job, then, is the story of the human race. It's both historically literal, I believe, and a grand parable. It's the real-life synopsis of humanity's fall: from bliss, to a painful experience with lots of unanswered questions, to a double blessing in the final chapter—all for the sake of a sacred demonstration of the worthiness of God.

God's question to the enemy was once, "Have you considered my servant Job?" The enemy lost the bet, and the Almighty's glory was displayed. Maybe sometimes God's question is, "Have you considered [insert your name]?" Is your suffering part of an unearthly showdown? Don't be offended if it is; rest assured that God's honor is well worth the trouble. He will see to that. We cannot charge him with selfishness if he makes it utterly worthwhile in the end.

But perhaps God's most in-your-face question to the enemy is now, "Have you considered Jesus?" There is absolutely nothing the adversary can say to that. His mouth is shut in shame, and God's mercy is displayed in splendor. Does that make God selfish? No one who has ever considered Jesus—including the enemy—could possibly say yes.

12

Unredeemed Suffering—
the Problem of Hell

*What if God, desiring to show his wrath and to make known
his power, has endured with much patience vessels of wrath
prepared for destruction . . . ?*

Romans 9:22

I was an impressionable seventeen-year-old, and I looked up
to my math teacher. He allowed quite a bit of dialogue in
class, even when it strayed from the subject of calculus. He
was especially cool for allowing Christian students to express
their views in an era when it was decidedly uncool to be a
Christian in a public school. So I was somewhat taken aback
when he interjected his own views into a conversation one
day. "I used to believe all of those things, just like you do.
Youth group, church every Sunday, the whole nine yards.
But I started to question it after a while. I just don't see how
a loving God could send people to hell."

I've heard it hundreds of times since, from high-minded religion columnists, from ivory-tower philosophers, even from people in the pew. "How can a loving God send people to hell?" That's the deepest core of the question of suffering. It has led some Christians to warp their creeds enough to include an unbiblical universal salvation; it has caused others to reject the faith altogether. Critics scoff at the seeming irreconcilability of a loving God and eternal torment. Believers have a hard time explaining it all; we just appeal to the authority of Scripture.

Unredeemed suffering is really the problem with the problem of evil. We grieve over the pains we experience now—the diseases, the agonizing losses, the death of our loved ones. But we can console ourselves with the knowledge that such losses are momentary and every tear will be wiped away in heaven. All religions stress the temporary nature of pain. They have to. The thought that it will never go away is too much to take.

For some, however, it never goes away. We might try to theologize hell away, but we can't accept the authority of Scripture and deny the reality of eternal torment. Jesus talked about hell a lot—more than heaven, in fact. If he didn't really say those things, we don't know what he said at all. If Jesus is truth, hell is real.

That hurts. We don't know what to do with that. We've been exploring an apologetic of pain that emphasizes God's ability to display his character on the stage of our suffering. Part of his display includes a day of wrath: "The LORD has made everything for its own purpose, even the wicked for the day of evil" (Prov. 16:4 NASB). When we're confronted with this unredeemed suffering—the torment that will not go away—we stall. People die and never know God. They languish in the outer darkness. What is worthwhile about that?

145

For them, nothing. That's the tragedy. God's offer of mercy is available to any who will receive it, but many will not. To accept it means to accept the sacrifice of his Messiah and to embrace that Messiah's authority, but we prefer to keep authority for ourselves, and we refuse to acknowledge our need for such a brutal, holy sacrifice. If we live without his sacrifice and authority, we die in our own insufficient obedience and under our own authority, and that won't get us very far. People all over this planet emphatically reject the Savior and then are offended when we say they aren't saved.

That is part of the evil in this world. We hold God at arm's length and resist his "intrusion" into our lives. That's what self-deification does; it places self-will on the throne of our hearts and does not give God his rightful place as Lord. We make ourselves our own gods and then wonder where God is when we experience pain. We try to arrange our own comfort and plan our own lives, but when things go awry, we shift sovereigns; we blame him and tell him we don't understand why he won't let things work out for us. Perhaps he is simply letting us experience the futility of our self-god. We think we can navigate the darkness of this world, but we can't. God lets us find that out. Sometimes we refuse to accept the truth of our rebellion for our entire lives. When that happens, there is little for God to do for us. He offered salvation; we didn't like what it implied and rejected it. How can he force us to accept what we so vigorously reject?

That's why there is hell. We like to think that only a very few really bad people go there, but that's just not consistent with the Bible. Hell is real, and its gates are wide. The way that leads to life is as narrow as a single Savior; "those who find it are few" (Matt. 7:14). When tender mercy has extended as far as hard hearts will let it, there is only one remaining option, and it's devastating.

Judgment Revealed

We can still apply the same argument to hell that we've applied to other suffering, in a sense. If God wants to use our suffering to reveal his character, then he can reveal himself as either merciful or just. "Mercy triumphs over judgment," says James 2:13; that's God's preference—to show mercy. But judgment is the other side of that coin. It too cannot be seen apart from a fallen world. It requires an object as much as mercy does. If God was ever going to reveal the holy, just, and wrathful side of his character in a way heaven had never seen, there would need to be a depraved, fallen creature to receive it. Our world is not unfamiliar with such creatures.

But that doesn't fully solve the problem, does it? God had presumably already expelled Lucifer and his followers from heaven. Judgment was not a hidden attribute of God. And couldn't judgment be well illustrated with a few high-profile victims rather than billions of anonymous ones? According to the Bible, multitudes will be cast into the outer darkness. The problem remains.

Paul struggled with the same problem. He attributed it to the sovereignty of God, which is pretty much all we can do. God will have mercy on whom he has mercy and harden whom he desires to harden (Rom. 9:18). He endured with much patience the vessels of wrath prepared for destruction. Why? So he might make known his glory through the vessels of mercy (Rom. 9:22–23). But why are there both vessels of mercy and vessels of wrath? And why are there relatively few of the former and so many of the latter? That isn't clearly answered for us. How desperately we wish it were!

We are assured that there is no injustice with God. We can accept that. But why would he tolerate the damnation of his creatures? Is there any glory in that?

Eternal, unredeemed suffering is not worthwhile at all for those who are its captives. But in the big picture, God's glory is maintained. If we remember that his glory is the highest possible value, the most worthwhile goal in the universe, then what cost could exceed it? God's creation, we must remind ourselves, is not all about us; it's all about him and the revelation of himself in the person of Jesus (Col. 1:16). He is extravagant in his invitation for us to join him in the celebration of his goodness and to marvel at his merciful character, but it is still all about him. He did not create the world to manifest the goodness of humanity. He created it to manifest himself and, in doing so, gave us the awesome privilege of being intimate with him in the fellowship of his Spirit.

This is the current of the universe. If we swim against it, we will suffer the consequences, and those consequences can be eternal. Does that detract from his glory? Only if the cost of many people suffering irreconcilably outweighs the value of many people fulfilling his glorious purpose. But it does not. He is honored by those who will receive his mercy, and no loss, however tragic and widespread, diminishes his honor. Paul's value system, while expressed in the context of his legalistic background, is an appropriate assessment of worth: "I count everything as loss because of the surpassing worth of knowing Christ Jesus my Lord" (Phil. 3:8). He meant it too, even when praying for this knowledge for others; in Romans 9, he wishes he himself could be cursed and cut off from Christ if that would save his kinsmen, for "to them belong . . . the glory, . . . the worship, and the promises" (v. 4). Human knowledge of God in Christ, corporately and individually, is infinitely valuable, and no one's suffering—in any amount—makes knowing him unworthwhile. The gains of mercy far outweigh the losses of condemnation.

We must remember that whether there is or is not a fallen world, there will be tragedy. In the absence of our brokenness, the tragedy is of an unrevealed God of mercy. He can never be known. His most winsome attributes can never become the basis of any heavenly fellowship. That is a greater tragedy than the existence of a broken world that will result in everlasting loss for many of its citizens. Our question is not so much about why God allowed this earthly tragedy to happen as it is about why he chose it over the alternative. And that's much more easily answered.

We still don't know all the mysteries of suffering, especially this one. But we know God is fair. He assures us of that. A passage in 2 Chronicles may give us a glimpse of God's character with regard to judgment: "[He] sent persistently to them by his messengers, because he had compassion on his people and on his dwelling place. But they kept mocking the messengers of God, despising his words and scoffing at his prophets, until the wrath of the LORD rose against his people, until there was no remedy" (36:15–16). Hell, ultimately, is the place of no remedy.

If finite minds have a hard time reconciling that with their sense of fairness, so be it. We do not know why hell is so final and why its capacity is so enormous, but we know it must exist if the justice of God and the redemption of a remnant are to be displayed. Other than that, we are just left to grieve over those who dwell there and to appreciate the one who saved us from it.

Yes, the unredeemed individual loses out. That is tragic. Jesus portrays God as a widow who relentlessly hunts for

149

her lost coin and as a shepherd who relentlessly pursues his lost sheep. He is clearly not oblivious to the tragedy of the individual. But for God's creation as a whole, the context of evil and suffering is infinitely worthwhile. It is a necessary background for redemption. It points to a beautiful Savior whose worth is unmatched.

13

When All Hell Breaks Loose

Your adversary the devil prowls around like a roaring lion, seeking someone to devour.

1 Peter 5:8

My wife and I had just prayed for a deeper experience with God and a new understanding of what it means for the Holy Spirit to fill our lives. Not only that, we were considering (and strongly leaning toward) applying to be involved in a new area of ministry among the many apartment dwellers in our city. We were also planning and praying about when to reapply to a missions agency that had put us on hold for a couple of years; we had it in our minds that we would go live overseas sometime in the foreseeable future. And as all of this was coming to a point of decision, my son had his accident. Over the next few weeks, it became clear: there would be no apartment ministry and no overseas missions for a long time. And if God wanted to give us a more intimate relationship with his Spirit, he would have to do that on his own. We were focused on a kid in a coma.

It really seemed that God had called us in the directions we were seeking. We had prayed and gotten some specific guidance. Why, then, was this insurmountable roadblock put in our way? We felt like Paul when he lamented to the Thessalonians, "We wanted to come to you—I, Paul, again and again—but Satan hindered us" (1 Thess. 2:18). It was pretty clear in that incident, and others before and since then, that we had an enemy.

Now, I don't mean to imply that my son's accident happened exclusively to hinder our ministry. The world doesn't revolve around me, and I know that. But I do believe that the enemy had a purpose in it—multiple purposes, in fact. He has exploited the situation in many ways and among many people, and it has become clear over time and in many instances that whenever God wants to do something in any of our lives, it isn't going to go uncontested.

I also don't mean to imply that God's ultimate will was thwarted in this situation. Just as Paul's unseen opposition steered him into other areas of opportunity, so did ours. And the prayer request we had made about having a deeper relationship with God was in large part answered through the circumstances we found ourselves in, not in spite of them. We don't understand how God's will and the enemy's opposition work together—it takes us back to that sovereignty question again—but they do. Different areas of ministry have opened up, and our experience of God has gotten deeper. Satan fights, and God wins. We've experienced both.

Yes, It's Personal

You can probably relate to stories like mine. You may have noticed that whenever you really begin to grow spiritually—you begin exploring God's direction for your life, make progress ridding yourself of a sinful tendency, or begin memorizing Scripture and integrating it into your life, for example—obstacles seem to come up alarmingly often. If you've been a child of God for long, if the body of Christ has been your home for any time at all, you know: evil is not just a force to explain. It is far more personal than that. Do we really think such well-crafted, specific attacks and temptations are some abstract concept that is part of the fabric of this existence? No, we are not harassed by a concept. We wrestle with the evil one.

Much of this book has depersonalized the problem, because this question that plagues us demands that we explain why God lets bad things happen. We affirm that he is sovereign and that some things that happen under his sovereignty seem to contradict his character. That's necessary for the sake of discussion, perhaps, but there is a more accurate way to state it. Our battle is "against the rulers, against the authorities, against the cosmic powers over this present darkness, against the spiritual forces of evil in the heavenly places" (Eph. 6:12). A better way to ask this question we've been discussing, then, is not "Why does God let bad things happen?" but "Why does God let the bad one get away with so many things?"

We do a disservice to the discussion when we depersonalize the problem to the point of never recognizing its source. In reality, we don't engage in a philosophy of evil; we fight against evil personalities. The difference is one of relevance. This struggle we all go through when we or our loved ones suffer is the product of living in a fallen world. But it is much more than that.

We live in a world that is under the pervasive influence of a relentless, malicious intelligence. God's creation has a jealous saboteur. We simply must acknowledge this if we are to bring any realism to the problem. It changes the nature of the fight, and, while it doesn't entirely exonerate God from a philosophical point of view, it does allow us to place the blame where it really belongs. Rebellion was allowed by God, but it was not generated by him.

I don't mean to imply that we deal only with the spirit world and never with the sinful nature we were born with or the natural consequences of a fallen world. Not every difficulty is prompted by some demonic agenda. Sometimes bad things happen because we live in a world of bad things. Sometimes natural disasters are natural. But most of us tend to err on the side of emphasizing naturalism in these things more often than on the side of emphasizing spiritualism. We need a reminder that this whole question of suffering began with a rebellious instigator. We need to understand that God does not govern a world in which evil just happened. This world is repeatedly raped, and it isn't by the dark side of a force or by negative vibes; there's a rapist.

The Bible rarely refers to evil as a concept. The temptation in the Garden of Eden came from a serpent, not a principle. Jesus never cast out a problem; he cast out spirits. He held conversations with them and called them by name. You can't do that with an abstract idea. When he taught the disciples to pray, he told them to ask God to deliver them from the evil one.[1] Jesus often referred to the prince of this world, the ruler of this world, the father of lies, and the original murderer. John spells it out for us: "The whole world lies in the power of the evil one" (1 John 5:19). Overwhelmingly, the Bible refers to wicked people and wicked powers more than impersonal wicked forces. The problem of pain is highly personal. We live in a broken world because someone broke it.

Why is this important to know? Because it is difficult to have a personal relationship with Jesus while having an abstract struggle with pain. Somehow, God is more comforting to us when we know we have an enemy rather than a problem. Just as our healer God becomes real to us only in the context of disease or injury, our warrior God, our Victor, our conquering King, only becomes real to us when we have an adversary with a personal agenda. That's not just good psychology; it's good hermeneutics and good theology. Actually, it's more than that. It's reality.

The rest of this book will continue to deal with the problem of evil as a philosophical issue, because that's how our world frames it for us and that's how sophisticates accuse God of negligence or of gross misrepresentation of his own character. But we know better. Our adversary runs wild on this planet, and the problem is not so much why God allows torment but why he tolerates the tormentor. Perhaps, as he did for the Israelites, he leaves the adversary in the land that we might be taught how to wage war against evil (see Judg. 3:2). Perhaps he is developing us in ways that the absence of evil could never do. Perhaps the give-and-take between disaster and deliverance is to be repeated so often that knowing the rescuer God becomes instinctive to us.

Regardless of why, when you feel like you are under attack, when all hell seems to be breaking loose against you, when temptations are coming from every direction, when you lie awake in the deep, dark night, wondering why everything seems to be an obstacle, remember the reality of the situation: this is personal.

14

Epicurus Answered

We have this treasure in jars of clay, to show that the surpassing power belongs to God and not to us. We are afflicted in every way, but not crushed; perplexed, but not driven to despair; persecuted, but not forsaken; struck down, but not destroyed; always carrying in the body the death of Jesus, so that the life of Jesus may also be manifested in our bodies.

2 Corinthians 4:7–10

Epicurus (and numerous philosophers and theologians since) maintained that the simultaneous existence of a good God, an all-powerful God, and rampant evil seems contradictory. The three-pronged problem seems to be intractable if we are to maintain our belief in the God of the Bible. Which of these points can be compromised? The Bible is extravagant in its affirmation of God's goodness and love and his majesty and power, and neither the Bible nor our experience will let us compromise the fact of evil. So how do we put our biblical understanding into philosophical terms that make sense?

We do not remove or compromise one of the conflicting elements; we add another. The three-element problem is only intractable when we hold human comfort and well-being to be paramount. Most of us approach life this way; the love and goodness of God imply to us that we will be well cared for and kept from ultimate harm. Epicurus certainly approached life with an ultimate regard for pleasure, which perhaps explains why he could not see beyond this problem as it is stated.

Let's review the holes in this oversimplified philosophy. We have seen from the Bible that there is a value in this universe higher than the well-being of humanity; it is the glory of God. If humanity were the ultimate value in this universe, then the problem could not be solved; God could not be both good and omnipotent in the face of evil. From this perspective, the welfare of human beings would be paramount. The problem wins, and our concept of God loses. If the ultimate value is God's glory, however, then it is entirely plausible that God's goodness and power can coexist with evil. Epicurus was wrong. Evil, while threatening the comfort level of humanity, can highlight God's character and his ways in a number of respects. Therefore, in order to solve this philosophical puzzle, we don't need to remove one of the three elements; we need to add a fourth—the glory of the God of love.

Consider the following illustration. I'm a fan of the game of football. Usually my team is out of contention by the time the play-offs roll around—but I'm still interested. Every year there are multiple teams fighting for multiple play-off spots, and that is fascinating to me. Why? Because there are always more teams than play-off spots. Suppose the last day of the season comes down to three teams fighting for the two final play-off berths. One of them will lose out. That goes unquestioned, doesn't it? There is no way to solve a problem of three teams and two play-off berths without one team being eliminated. The fans of one team will have to make an involuntary sacrifice; all three interests cannot be appeased simultaneously. And if football were all about the teams, I would lament the sacrifice, and that would be the end of it.

But it isn't. Football is about the game. I'm still interested in watching those three teams fight for survival, but not because I love those teams and will be heartbroken when one of them falls. I'm still interested because I love the game. That's my overriding concern that eliminates the tragedy of the individual teams. The interests of the three teams cannot coexist. But throw in a fourth element—the glory of the game itself—and it changes everything. That cutthroat competition on the last day of the season tells me a lot about the character of the teams, and it defines for me the character of the game. If that tension were not there, I wouldn't be interested at all, and I'd know very little about football.

Now, that's a crude illustration, and I don't mean to imply that God's character is a cutthroat competition or that the fate of billions of souls is a sport. It isn't; the stakes are much higher than that. But that dynamic is in operation when we approach the three-pronged problem of evil. Yes, one of those elements must be sacrificed if human comfort is the priority; one of those "teams" will lose. But that's only the view from the level of those three elements. Rise above them, and look at the overall picture: God is glorified because his character is revealed in ways it never would have been if evil did not exist. Goodness and power and evil will bow to that higher good. But the fourth consideration overrides them all. It means everything.

Consider another, gentler illustration. Our environment too has contradictory elements within it, even while it functions powerfully and beautifully as a system. For example, from ground level, at any given point in time, we cannot maintain the simultaneous existence of rain, wind, and sun. If it's rainy and windy, it isn't sunny. If it's sunny and windy, it isn't rainy. If it's sunny and rainy—the rarest of the three combinations because it requires that the rain fall and the sun shine from different angles—it isn't windy. If it's windy at all, the clouds either move in front of the sun or the rain is driven away from us. But rain and wind and sun coexist in the overall environment, because that's how the environment is maintained and stays in balance. It's actually beautiful that way. Sacrifice any one of those elements, and the glory of creation suffers. But ask any one of us how they can simultaneously coexist, and we can't imagine it. We can't see it from our level, at least not for longer than a moment. Each of us would probably compromise one of those elements if we could—dismal rain or harsh sun, for example. But add an overriding consideration to the mix, and they all make sense together. At an elemental level, the conditions don't work. At a systemic level—the view from a hundred miles up—they work perfectly. The gentle and harsh elements serve a higher environmental cause, and the cause is extremely worthwhile.

Yet another illustration: Those with an ear for music have certainly heard three keys of a piano played simultaneously to make an absolutely abhorrent sound. Standing alone, the dissonance is brutal on the ears. In passing (which the problem of evil certainly is), the ugly chord can serve a beautiful purpose. The difference is in realizing the context, understanding that there is a greater concern than the isolated elements of the chord. The dissonance will be resolved, and the resolution is actually more satisfying because of the dissonance that set it up. There is a work of art at stake here, a beautiful piece of music. That higher purpose defined, the ugliness below can be better understood and tolerated.

A Higher Purpose

Yes, these are all crude illustrations, and they certainly aren't exact parallels, but they do point to a dynamic: it is possible for things to contradict each other at an elemental level while serving a systemic goal. Sometimes three elements of a problem are in conflict, but when we consider a higher purpose to them all, they come into focus. They only contradict one another when all three points are considered to have equal weight. Add a much weightier consideration, however—a coherent whole that is more than the sum of its parts—and the contradiction begins to fade. The dissonance at the lower level where the problem is becomes a crucial part of the entirety, serving a greater purpose and highlighting a more beautiful resolution.

Do you see how this changes everything? The question is no longer, How can a loving God let this happen? The question, variously phrased, is, What does this horror show us about God? What can we discover of him in the context of our pain? How does he want to display himself in this dire situation? The best answer to the question that has been gnawing at us from day one of our lives and from chapter one this book is not an answer at all; it is a different set of questions.

While we've been picking out incidents of tragedy—and granted, there are many to choose from—God has been urging us to wait for the resolution. He has given us sweeping promises like Romans 8:28: "For those who love God all things work together for good, for those who are called according to his purpose." He calls us toward faith and hope and all those things that seem so abstract when we first read them. He asks us not to wield suffering as an intellectual weapon against him but to invite him into it wherever we see it. Once we change the question to reflect what is really going on in this universe—from how he could let it happen to what it might show us about him—then we can at least begin to approach an answer. When the world is all about us, the question about evil lingers, pesters, and nags. When the world is all about God, the question loses its validity. It changes; we have to ask a different one. And things begin to make some sense.

Living with the Mystery

Has it ever bothered you that God never really answered Job's questions? Instead, he delivered a defense of his sovereignty and an overwhelming assertion of his wisdom. Rather than a point-by-point analysis of where Job was faulty in his thinking, God eliminated the need for the questions to begin with. His answer was that he is sovereign and good and wise and well aware of the situation. That's all Job really needed to know.

We don't like that answer, do we? Perhaps we, like Job, have made understanding our idol. Perhaps we, like Job, felt that we were doing a good job handling everything—worshiping God the right way, living with integrity, looking out for our relationships—and that evil and suffering came along and messed up our formula. We lost our sense of control.

That happens whenever some "together" person faces a crisis. I've seen it over and over again, and so have you. So-and-so had it all—that is, until he (or she) was diagnosed with cancer and it turned his (or her) life upside down. And we can't always chalk that up to someone who put faith in possessions and circumstances and was given a crisis to rearrange his or her priorities. Even in the spiritual realm of having it all together, we sometimes see young, promising missionaries die in their first year on the field or have to return home because of some family tragedy. No matter how we spin it, sometimes there is simply no visible, discernible answer. It's a mystery.

The problem with us humans is that we want to reduce our faith, or even our whole lives, to a formula. And while God never tells us to lose our curiosity and inquisitive nature—he gave those to us, after all—he does compel us to live with some level of mystery. Adam and Eve were never told why the tree's fruit was forbidden, just that it was. Joseph was never given an up-front explanation of his trials so he wouldn't stress over them as he was going through them. David never really got an explanation about Saul's zealous and jealous pursuit of him for all those years. Even the disciples were in the dark until after the resurrection, wondering for days if they had wasted an awful lot of time with that Nazarene.

God gives us hints and glimpses of eternity and its truths, but he also expects us to live with a sense of mystery. After all, how are finite minds going to comprehend a complete unfolding of it anyway? We who need handles and control are striving after something we were never designed to handle or control. Eternal explanations belong to infinite minds, and there's only one of those. Our job is to trust him.

Perhaps you've found that difficult in a time of crisis. Welcome to life in this fallen world. You want things to make sense, and sometimes they don't. When that happens, try this exercise: instead of changing your spin on God in order to make sense of the circumstances, change your spin on the circumstances in order to make sense of God. The first course of action—trying to adapt God to fit the circumstances—is the stuff of idolatry. It's a natural human response, but it's not allowed. The second course of action is biblical. We are always allowed to interpret circumstances according to who we know God to be.

So when you're suffering, do your best to consciously adapt your interpretation of circumstances to fit the biblical picture of God rather than change your interpretation of God to fit the picture of your circumstances. Rehearse his mercies often, naming them in your mind—or out loud, if that helps. Be diligent and even aggressive to remind yourself that because God is loving and powerful, evil has a worthwhile purpose in your life. And remember that one day you'll see it.

PART 4

THE PRIZE

. . . in order to make known the riches of his glory for vessels of mercy.

Romans 9:23

15

Spiritual Street Children

*Blessed be the God and Father of our Lord Jesus Christ, the
Father of mercies and God of all comfort, who comforts us
in all our affliction.*

2 Corinthians 1:3–4

Most of the really large cities in third-world countries have
a chronic social problem: street children. It's easy to be an-
noyed by them. They can pick your pocket or even endanger
your life. They've grown up in the city, and they are masters
of the street culture. They have no home but the sidewalk,
and they have no plan but survival.

Get beyond the annoyance, however, and you can't help
but be devastated by their stories. Most of them were brought
into the city by their parents and just left there. Why? Kids
cost money to support. Many families don't have money.
It's that simple.

I remember hearing one such story from a veteran missionary giving a presentation before a group of missionary candidates. She told of a four-year-old boy who came to the city one day with his father. She told of the harsh words of the father, who coldly informed his child that he would be on his own now. And the father just walked away.

I struggled to hold back tears, but I couldn't. I have a four-year-old. I can't imagine the horror on his face if I were to walk away, telling him he was on his own in a big city. He depends on me! He can't even tie his shoes. He needs love and food and playtime and lessons on life and everything. But in this broken world, four-year-olds in big cities grow up alone on the streets because their dads leave them there. Such fathers are the complete antithesis of the prodigal son's father. I can't get over the image of a small child standing on a street corner, watching the only one he ever trusted walk away. To me, it is the ultimate visual illustration behind our nagging questions about evil. It just isn't right.

What do we tell these abandoned children? That their abandonment is part of a big plan to reveal God's glory? The biblical answer to evil is logical, but what does cold logic do for an emotionally devastated preschooler?

Indeed, what do we tell the Ethiopian woman who has just watched her child die of starvation, or the Bangladeshi whose family and possessions went the way of the last flood? What do we tell the person who is in the late stages of a battle with cancer that has lasted way too long? How about the innocent person who has lost his life savings in an unjust lawsuit? And the teenager who is so lonely that all she wants to do is jump off a bridge? The families of the schoolchildren who were blown to pieces by the terrorist's bomb? The parents of the terrorist?

Are we to say that in this world of murder, famine, corporate greed, exploitation, loneliness, genocide, despair, war, deception, betrayal, theft, intimidation, self-exaltation, terrorism, earthquakes, cancer, AIDS, divorce, anthrax, and offensive insults—and that's clearly only a partial list—that a tidy theology of the glory of God is going to make things better? In the storied tradition of all who have tried to reconcile the love and power of God with the problem of evil, let me give a completely ambiguous answer: Yes. And no.

Here's what I mean. In the nuts and bolts of disaster, we feel pain. Our crises are not quickly resolved by smooth theologies. I do believe that the cautions against pat answers are getting tired; sometimes the answers are really there. But that doesn't mean the comfort is always instantaneous or that the answers take away the pain. They don't. Those who lose their children to starvation will grieve. They will not care, at least for the moment, about the glory of God and his ultimate plan to reveal himself as merciful. At that moment, mercy seems far, far away. When we cry out to God in unspeakable anguish, "Why, why, why?" it's OK. Even Jesus experienced such anguish. We don't get slapped on the wrist for being theologically uninformed. We're allowed to feel pain and to suffer. We would not be fallen humans in a broken world if we did not feel such things. We would not have been made in the image of the God who knows grief.

The theological answers to the problem of evil do not deny that the pain and suffering are real. In fact, they *depend* on the pain and suffering being intensely real. God's mercy means nothing if the need for it is quick, painless, or superficial. His tender comfort and the healing of our wounds are irrelevant when there is nothing excruciating to address. The comfort of God's character is never legitimate unless the anguish he calms is also legitimate.

The point is that in the midst of our suffering, God is there. He reveals himself in ways we never could have known in Eden. His compassion fills the hole in our heart that was left when we were abandoned or betrayed by a loved one. His love speaks into the emptiness we feel when our best friend dies. His promise is the only thing we have to hold on to when we're threatened by our own terminal disease.

No, the theological answers don't make it all better. But they are still answers. In every situation in which we suffer, there is something of God to experience. That doesn't mean everyone who suffers will experience him, but the relationship is nevertheless available to all. When we hurt, we must go searching. God has some comfort, some promise, some companionship, often even some miracle to give us. If our earthly fathers leave us as helpless children on the streets of Lima or Manila or wherever, the Father of the prodigal son can come running in. It takes time and a faithful church to demonstrate the glory of the running Father, but he is available if we'll present him as such. Make no mistake, the context in which we learn of him is absolutely agonizing. But in that agonizing context, *we can learn of him!*

Is that a pat answer? So be it. Just because the pain is real doesn't mean the answers aren't. No, they aren't the quick fix we wish for. But they are authentic. The God who shows up in our suffering, if we will let him, is genuine. Our hurts can drive us into his presence and his purpose. When we let them, we become participants in the divine drama that will forever thrill our hearts. We are promised that the treasure we gain in knowing more of him will far outweigh the pain that drove us there. In the nuts and bolts of crisis, let that be of some comfort.

Whispers, Shouts, and the Judges Enigma

In their distress [they will] earnestly seek me.

Hosea 5:15

As spiritual street children focused on survival, we often let the forces of our environment determine our direction. So it was in the book of Judges, where it's easy to discern a pattern: human beings desire God only when we're in trouble. That statement probably can't be universally applied; sometimes we do seek God when all is well. But it's exceptional when we do. Normally, people don't begin to look for God until their need for him has been made obvious.

The cycle in Judges is almost amusing. It begins in chapter 2, when Joshua's generation is dead and gone. "The people of Israel did what was evil in the sight of the LORD and served the Baals" (v. 11). Then when they "cried out to the LORD, the LORD raised up a deliverer" (3:9). We see the pattern again in verses 12 and 15 of chapter 3; then in 4:1, 3; then in verses 1 and 6 of chapter 6; then in 8:33; then in verses 6 and 16 of chapter 10; then in 13:1; and so on. It amazes us until we realize we're just like that. When things are going well, we let God become peripheral to our lives. As he becomes peripheral, life gets out of control. Then we cry like the Israelites. We lift up Gideon's lament.

You'll perhaps remember Gideon as one of Israel's judges. Israel was in the middle of one of its periods of doing "evil in the sight of the LORD." That usually means they had ceased their obedience to God's law and redirected their worship away from the one who had delivered them from Egypt, sustained them in the wilderness, and led them to victory in the Promised Land with so many miracles and awe-inspiring blessings. Instead, they worshiped various idols associated with the tribal religions of their adversaries. They bowed before the Baals and the Asherim of the Canaanites, participating in fertility rituals and relying on wood and stone for deliverance and sustenance. God's beloved, chosen people sometimes let gross sexual perversion and child sacrifice become a part of their spiritual adultery.

God often does not hesitate to turn us over to the gods we have chosen. The Israelites found themselves invaded by Midianites, Amalekites, and other eastern peoples during their apostasy. The Baals apparently couldn't deliver, so Israel cried out (again) for God to help them. In his mercy, God came to deliver. As we saw in chapter 10 of this book, he announced to Gideon that he was with his people. "If the LORD is with us," Gideon answered, "why then has all this happened to us? And where are all his wonderful deeds that our fathers recounted to us, saying, 'Did not the LORD bring us up from Egypt?' But now the LORD has forsaken us and given us into the hand of Midian" (Judg. 6:13).

We can relate. We live on a rebellious planet, and we have participated in the rebellion. We have sought our own interests and neglected our Creator, and now our planet is reeling. We have lived for self. We have gotten into trouble. We hurt. We are enslaved by conflict, by debt, by disease, by death, by a whole host of other invaders. And from the midst of this human rebellion, we cry out to God. "Why has all this happened? Where are you? Where are all the wonders we've heard about? Why have you abandoned us?" We marvel that he has not become the heavenly enabler, feeding us in our filthy diet of idolatry. While God is telling us that he is coming to help us in spite of ourselves, we are asking him where he has been.

C. S. Lewis puts the answer as succinctly as any. "God whispers to us in our pleasures, speaks to us in our conscience, but shouts in our pains; it is his megaphone to rouse a deaf world."[1] That's one very valid answer to our suffering. Ever since Eden, where God once walked with us freely and openly, we've hidden in the bushes. We avoid him because we're very aware of our shame and guilt when he's around. And when things are going well, what reason do we have not to avoid him? We may quietly thank him sometimes as he whispers his pleasure to us, but we don't want to get too close. So he lets us suffer. It's mercy, really. It's how he brings us back into his presence. If we won't draw close to him in our comfort, he'll drive us to him with our pain.

Not all suffering is a direct result of our waywardness and a direct prompt to get back to our God hunger, but some of it is. Our desires normally speak more loudly to us than any other voice. If our desires are fulfilled by our own ingenuity, God will put us in places of greater need until we have to have him. We're dealing with a God who means to have a relationship with his creation—he openly admits that he's a jealous God—and he'll allow us a great deal of discomfort if that's what we need to seek his presence.

The Judges phenomenon is pretty simple. In the post-fall human experience, ease equals apostasy and pain equals a desire for God. It's almost mathematical in its precision. Between Eden and the kingdom of God, we need pain. Without it we fall under the illusion that all might be well in this broken world. Pain accurately represents our condition and breaks the spell of the illusion. It points us in the right direction.

True Value

That brings us back to the value of suffering vis-à-vis the value of God. Do we really not understand how a loving God can let us hurt? Not only do we start to cry out to him in our pain, but we go to extraordinary lengths to find him.

"When your judgments are in the earth, the inhabitants of the world learn righteousness" (Isa. 26:9). Many people have read the entire Bible for the first time on their deathbeds. Many have accepted the salvation of Jesus as bullets flew over their heads. Many have sought God only when they've needed deliverance or healing. That's OK. He'll take that, at least as a start. Sometimes my children come to me only because they want something. I'm not happy with that as a permanent condition, but I'll take it on occasion. I'd rather have that than their complete absence. So what if they're just using me? It gives me a foot into the door of their hearts.

Our need often gives God a foot into the door of our hearts. We can ask why about our pain until we're blue in the face, but if it drives us to God, it's worthwhile. It's not barely worthwhile, not just a little worthwhile, but ultimately worthwhile—by a long shot. There is great value in it. It reveals God not just to a watching world but also to us. Who cares how much it costs? If it turns us to him, it's a small price to pay.

You may recall God's anger at the Israelites' complaints as they wandered through the wilderness. They were complaining in the face of God's merciful deliverance and in the context of his miraculous providence. They thought somehow that they were getting the raw end of the deal. When we focus on our troubles and forget the redemptive work of God in our lives—and specifically the redemptive work of God through our suffering—we grumble about his dealings with us. All the while, we're grumbling about the merciful work he does to change us.

C. S. Lewis was right: God shouts to us in our pain. When the kingdom comes in all its fullness, we'll remember in the megaphone of God the heart of our sacred suitor, not the discomfort of the pain. We'll be grateful for his ear-shattering shouts, just as the Israelites were, in retrospect, grateful for the invaders who prompted them to cry out to God. Through their painful pleas, a nation was preserved for God's own revelation. Through ours, so are we.

16

A Ministry of Reconciliation

All this is from God, who through Christ reconciled us to himself and gave us the ministry of reconciliation.

2 Corinthians 5:18

Many times when we see others in the crucible of life, we stand gazing at God to see what he'll do to reveal himself. We wonder what his response will be. Perhaps if we linger long enough, we'll hear the prompting of the Spirit within us: "You *are* the response of God."

No, we're not the sum total of God's response to our needy world—he's the one who can do miracles, not us. But if we are members of the body of Christ, then we are a substantial part of his presence here. We don't need to stand idly by, waiting to see how God will deliver. Often he will deliver through us, or at least use us in the process. We're conduits of his power and mercy to a hurting world. We have been comforted in order to give comfort. If suffering is the stage for God's glory, we are his supporting cast.

Not many Christians understand that. We hurt, and we cry out to God, and we wait for his answer. Do we not remember that when God answers, he often answers through other members of the body? The God of the Old Testament—Jehovah-Jireh, our Provider; Jehovah-Nissi, our Banner; Jehovah-Rapha, our Healer; the God who identifies himself as Warrior, Shield, Refuge, Redeemer, and more—this is the God who no longer dwells in a tabernacle or in a temple. He dwells in us. Those who are filled with the Holy Spirit will, without exception, do things that characterize the ministry of God. We will show mercy, we will help heal, we will help provide, we will help fight, and we will forgive.

The merciful characteristics of God are not revealed only in this suffering world; they are revealed through his people. Have you ever noticed that the lists of gifts and fruits of the Spirit in the New Testament correspond remarkably with the revelation of God's mercies in the Old Testament? Some have gifts of healing; God is our Healer (Exod. 15:26). Some have gifts of helping; God is our Helper (Deut. 33:29). Some teach, discern, prophesy, impart wisdom; all throughout the Bible, God teaches, grants discernment, inspires prophecy, and imparts wisdom. The description of him as he passes by Moses, showing his servant his glory, is a pretty good description of what we expect Spirit-filled believers to be like: "merciful and gracious, slow to anger, and abounding in steadfast love and faithfulness, keeping steadfast love for thousands, forgiving iniquity and transgression and sin" (Exod. 34:6–7).

There's a reason for the correlation. It is no coincidence that those who believe in God by faith in Jesus begin to take on the character of God in Jesus. We are in a painful process of being conformed to the image of Christ. That's God's goal for us—that we would look like Jesus. When we expect God to demonstrate his glory in a world of suffering, we have to expect to be a part of his demonstration. The rescuer God lets us participate in his glory; we become rescuing people.

It really doesn't take much scanning of the Scriptures to see this. Paul is perhaps most explicit: "In Christ God was reconciling the world to himself, not counting their trespasses against them" (2 Cor. 5:19). All the pain of this world, all of its fallenness and brokenness, has provided a platform for a merciful God to stand on and show himself. He has revealed his once hidden characteristics. But it does not end there, with the grand demonstration of the suffering servant Jesus. Paul finishes the verse: ". . . and entrusting to us the message of reconciliation."

Do you see the importance of that role? Not only is our suffering redeemable as a context for the divine glory, but we become participants in that glory! The pain of this world becomes the platform for God *and* for all those who are called by him, who love him, who are known by his name. The God who reaches from heaven with a merciful hand to show who he really is in all his glory does not often do so independently from his creation. He does it through us! We become the merciful hand of God.

Perhaps that is why Jesus is so intent on linking the mercy we receive with the mercy we give. Those who are merciful will receive mercy. Those who forgive will be forgiven. Those who are relieved of enormous debts only to go out and demand payment from all of their small debtors are those who just have not understood. The once hidden attributes of God have now been displayed on the stage of this world. If we've seen them, we'll live them; if we haven't, we won't.

Think of some of the most dedicated ministers you know. The great pulpit preachers probably benefited greatly from effective pulpit preaching early in their lives. Many of the people who have ministries with prostitutes or drug addicts came out of such bondage themselves. Many of those who relieve hunger were once hungry. Many of those who are Christian apologists once fought the evidence for the truth. The cycle of mercy isn't random or coincidental. There's a purpose in God's redeeming needy people from all their troubles and then using them as instruments in the redemption of other needy people. His transformed creation becomes a reflection of him.

That is why a suffering church is usually a vibrant and growing church. Evil and pain provide the context in which God's character can be most visibly demonstrated. Let history be our teacher: the first-century church, the Chinese church, the Sudanese church—this is where the gospel is most clearly revealed, first to its members and then to those to whom they minister. Why? The mercy of God shows up in our pain, our patience, our endurance, and our deliverance.

Churches that thrive in the midst of suffering are not unique to repressive, anti-Christian societies—or at least they don't have to be. Those churches suffer visibly in ways that churches in most of Western culture do not, but we have our sufferings as well. We have members who suffer from cancers and strokes, members who struggle with broken relationships, members who have fought hard to resist the basest temptations and have sometimes failed, members who have been abused, and members who have gone through just about every internal suffering imaginable, as well as much external pain. It's a horrible shame, a huge distortion of the Christian gospel about the God who rescues, that we often handle our wounded so roughly and carelessly that they leave the church with greater wounds than they came in with. Churches are to be places where the wounded can rest and heal, and the reason is more than just for the sake of the wounded. The reason is so that the rescuing, delivering, healing, saving, comforting, merciful God can demonstrate himself through his body and be glorified as a Rescuer, a Deliverer, a Healer, a Savior, a Comforter, and a Giver of great mercy.

Churches should look a lot like God. Our discipleship isn't about being conformed to his character in order to please his high standards; it's about being conformed to his character to demonstrate his character. That's where glory comes from. That's why this world was created and allowed to fall. Churches should be places where every hidden attribute of God is now displayed.

Jesus on the Jericho Road

Jesus told a now familiar parable about a good Samaritan who helped a neighbor in need. We often get the surface meaning of this story: we are to be more like the Samaritan, who wasn't expected to show mercy but did, rather than the religious leaders, who were expected to show mercy but didn't. But some take a different approach to the parable. Instead of putting yourself in the place of the priest or the Levite or the Samaritan, read it from the perspective of the victim. That's who we really are, you know—dying, ignored victims by the side of the Jericho road. But Jesus didn't ignore us; he saved us. He picked us up, took us to the inn, and paid the innkeeper to take care of us. He was the good neighbor. Now he gives us an imperative: "You go, and do likewise" (Luke 10:37).

That's the essence of this broken creation. It was fallen and dying by the side of the road. God sent Jesus to save it at great cost. In the context of suffering, the mercy of the Father and the Son is displayed for all heaven, hell, and earth to see. But the story doesn't end there. There is more to this divine show of mercy. It calls for participants—you and me. People who will reflect what they have discovered about the manifold character of God. People who will put feet on their suffering, who—like God—will turn pain into an occasion for honor. People who understand what it means to demonstrate glory in a dark, dark world. People who will see what God has done . . . and go and do the same.

The Finished Product

> You have been grieved by various trials, so that the tested genuineness of your faith—more precious than gold that perishes though it is tested by fire—may be found to result in praise and glory and honor at the revelation of Jesus Christ.
>
> 1 Peter 1:6–7

One illustration fairly common among pastors who preach on the problem of pain is of a famous sculptor (let's say Michelangelo) working on his most beautiful sculpture (let's say *David*). Michelangelo begins with a block of stone. He chisels and hammers and chips away and sands and grinds until all that's left is the magnificent work of art we know as *David*. The preacher will usually compare this chipping-away process to the work suffering does in our lives. God uses our pain to strip us of all our false props, expose our idolatrous souls until we're naked before him, and infuse his life into the raw material that is us. By such painful processes we are conformed to the image of Christ—it is actually Jesus who is the Artist's model for the sculpture.

We are told early on in Scripture that we are made in God's image. The rebellion in the garden shattered that image, but it is still there. Salvation by faith in Jesus—he who is the *exact* image of God (Heb. 1:3)—begins the restoration process, and the final product is better than it was before. We glorify God because of his amazing grace in the process. He shares his glory with us in at least two ways: we become the demonstration of his character on earth, and we become the eternal testimony of his mercies. All of heaven and earth will rejoice at the grand finale, even while hell gnashes its teeth. The party celebrating God's mercies will never end.

The sad part of the earth story is that there is much suffering, at least for some individuals, that does not end with a party. The judgments of God are righteous, and we will be glad for that. And in the big picture, the demonstration of wrath will serve God's purposes as well as the demonstration of his mercy. Meanwhile, we need not fear ultimate disaster on a cosmic scale. God's goodness will be preserved. But there is a pang of sadness for all who won't celebrate at the final revelation of Jesus.

It is amazing to see the diverse effects pain has on people. It has turned some into skeptics and atheists. It has turned others into agnostic existentialists who wonder if there is any meaning to it all. Crowds of nameless, emotionless faces walking the rainy streets of Paris or London in depressing European films are perfect illustrations of a traumatized creation. Angst is real, and its underlying assumption is that pain is unredeemable. Nothing is left but fatalistic resignation.

But suffering has also had the opposite effect on people. Some have been stripped of everything that doesn't fit with the final image, just like the block of marble. The result is faith. The painful process that exposes the bare nerves of the soul has led many people straight to God, just as it has led many in the opposite direction. It's hard to understand the diversity. What makes the difference between a hopeless existentialist in a concentration camp and a Corrie ten Boom who comes out of it with unshakable confidence in the Almighty? They've experienced the same tragedies, witnessed the same horrors. One walks away an ardent atheist, the other an impassioned believer. What makes the difference?

Perhaps that's the point of pain to begin with, at least from a human perspective. Not only does its stage become the platform for God's mercies, but it becomes the test of faith that they exist. God's mercies are revealed—at least eventually—to those who count on them. They are forever hidden from those who cannot bring themselves to believe the promise. Just like Job, we are tested, sifted, shaken to our core to see what comes out. If faith survives that trial, it brings us into the final celebration. If faith doesn't survive the test, it wasn't real and there is no final celebration. As in the parable of the talents in Matthew 25, to everyone who has, more will be given; from everyone who does not have, all will be taken away. If the principle applies to eternal investments, it might well apply to faith in the mercies of God. In the end we will either rejoice with inexpressible, ecstatic joy or weep and gnash our teeth. There is no middle alternative.

Pain has a remarkable way of driving us in either of those directions. It removes the pretense of the middle alternative. Those who suffer know: the illusion of indifference cannot withstand the crucible. We will either fix our hope completely on eternal truths or abandon them altogether, hopeless, bitter, and afraid. There is no room for apathy in suffering. It is the great divider.

That's a gift, really. Lukewarmness is a dangerous condition. When we are lukewarm in our faith, we have the illusion of safety, but we may be just as faithless as the atheist. Suffering is a blessing from God that will drive us either passionately and desperately toward him or hopelessly away from him. The lukewarm and the hopeless may have the same status before him, so there is really nothing to lose in the proposition; we can only come closer into his presence. If you've suffered—and if you're human, you have—then you can relate: there is no more comforting place to be when you hurt than in his presence. Suffering is a gift that strips us of apathy and indifference and sends us on a diligent search for the heart of God. Blessed are those who believe they will find it.

I don't believe it's a coincidence when aspiring pastors, missionaries, church planters, ministry founders, and any other folks who want to bear much fruit for God begin their ministry with near-fatal setbacks. The death of a loved one, a crippling disease, an irreconcilable conflict—these are Satan's plans to shatter us and God's designs to sculpt us. Those who want to display the Sustainer often must carry deep wounds with them throughout their lives. Why? So he can be seen in them. "We have this treasure in jars of clay, to show that the surpassing power belongs to God and to us. . . . For we who live are always being given over to death for Jesus' sake, so that the life of Jesus also may be manifested in our mortal flesh" (2 Cor. 4:7, 11).

Holy Wound Bearers

God's character comes through in a special way when we bear the marks of suffering. They are holes that only he can fill. The seeds of mercy are best sown on a ground of woundedness. And the wound bearers who have found this mercy are best qualified to sow it in other fields. We can wear our pain as a badge of honor; he has chosen us in order to reveal himself.

We will probably never get to the point where we're glad we get to suffer. It isn't natural for us to enjoy that part of our existence, even though James tells us to "count it all joy" (1:2). When life hurts, we want to curl up and die. The fires of the crucible can be cruel, and though we can find joy in the midst of them, we can never really relish them. But we *can* get to the point where we appreciate the role we play in the divine demonstration of mercy. We can take heart in the fact that God either has already or will one day show himself in our pain.

We see that already, don't we? I know someone who has lived a near-perfect moral life. He sings praises for God's ability to sanctify, to make holy and pure. I'm sure in his heart that's a profound praise, but I have seen only the sterling example of this man's life. I've never seen him trapped deep in his sin, so his praises, while legitimate and wonderful, aren't that much of a testimony to me. On the other hand, I know someone who was deeply mired in impurity, struggling to get out of his sinfulness and usually losing the struggle. Over time, through much prayer and counsel, God cleansed him and made him pure. His spotlessness is remarkable, a stark contrast to his former life. When he praises God for his sanctifying power, it amazes me. I see the power of God in those praises, because I know the story. It's a spiritual rags-to-riches story, and the only explanation is God. His holiness and his power are greatly glorified.

Radical transformation has a way of not only making God's glory seen in one instance but also reproducing that marvelous spectacle again and again. There's a ministry in the red-light districts of Bangkok, for example, that rescues young women who have been sold into what amounts to slavery. They are given temporary jobs and a lot of counsel and support. As they withdraw from the culture of the sex trade and become involved in the culture of the ministry, they often play the role of an intermediary in helping others out. They become rescuers, living parables of what God can do to change lives.

Many evangelicals know the story of Charles Colson, implicated in the Watergate scandal and imprisoned shortly thereafter. By Colson's own admission, he was a master of political hardball, able to manipulate and execute the dirty tricks that often come with the political process. But in the aftermath of the scandal, Colson became a Christian. He served his time, and as he did so, he saw a need among prisoners that churches could fill. His ministry, Prison Fellowship, is now the world's largest outreach to prisoners, with forty thousand prison ministry volunteers in over a hundred countries. Why does that wonderful ministry exist? Because one man who had been involved in some very ugly business in the 1970s went to prison for his crimes and God showed up in mercy.

That dynamic is repeated often: ministries to orphans, divorcees, homosexuals, the homeless, and so on are often begun by those who were once orphaned, divorced, homosexual, or homeless. Those whose needs were met by God become the means to administer God's love to others. The pain of our crises demonstrates something previously known only at a distance about God. It takes propositional truth—facts about God—and turns it into experiential knowledge. The difference is precious. The wound bearers become wound dressers, and mercy is made manifest.

The fact is that we see God most clearly, and praise him most profusely, in the context and aftermath of our brokenness, in its extremes. My tendency is to pray for healing every time I have a head cold, but when you ask me about God showing up in my need, I'll point you to the time my son was in a coma for six weeks on the brink of death and God spared his life. Our desperation helps us see him, and the deeper the desperation, the better we eventually see. We certainly don't need to accentuate or magnify our sin and sickness to glorify God; it's already bad enough. But we can take heart that there is something of him to be seen in our pitiful condition. And in our need, it's our job to seek that revelation, for his sake and for ours.

That means that when a spouse has left you, a cancer is eating at you, a precious part of your life has been stolen from you, you've been betrayed, or you've suffered any other catastrophe, there's a Godward response you can embrace, if you'll so choose. It's perfectly normal to get discouraged, even depressed, over these things. It's natural to be devastated. But it's tragic to remain devastated. When you're picking up the pieces and trying to move on, consider asking God what part of himself he wants to show in your life. It may or may not be the attribute you most hope for at the moment, but it will be something, and it will be meaningful. Down the road you'll see that your trial and your pain have brought you closer to God than you ever could have been otherwise and, in fact, have prepared you to be a minister of his mercy. Yes, your trial will make you tougher and more patient and of a stronger character, but character development is probably evident even in someone with no faith at all. Your request of your Father will take you farther, beyond the chiseled features of a soul who's been through a lot. It will draw you into his presence, where his character is seen, his comfort is felt, and his power is believable. It will, in short, reveal God—not just to you but through you.

The Ultimate Example

If we really want to see how God reveals himself in suffering, the ultimate example is the incarnation. Jesus suffered. He hungered, he thirsted, he wept, he was slandered and slighted, beaten and abused. He was unjustly tortured and executed. And still today we call him the ultimate revelation of God, the "exact imprint of his nature" (Heb. 1:3), the "image of the invisible God" (Col. 1:15). Doesn't that latter verse affirm the whole point of this discussion? The invisible is made visible; the hidden characteristics of mercy—forgiveness, unconditional love, healing, restoration, reconciliation, deliverance, and so on—stepped into a fallen world in a manger in Bethlehem.

If we are his disciples, these very attributes are also to be displayed in us. We are not just victims of suffering. We are the visible response of God in the midst of it. In this context of evil and pain, Ephesians 2:6–7 takes on a different, fuller meaning: "[God] raised us up with him and seated us with him in the heavenly places in Christ Jesus, *so that in the coming ages he might show the immeasurable riches of his grace.*" The context of fallenness has a purpose; it is a demonstration of who God is. Jesus is the prototype; we are the evidence and continuation of the theme.

A New Reformation

I believe there needs to be a reformation in the church—not an institutional or doctrinal reformation but a reformation in the way Christians think about suffering. Instead of falling into the "why me" syndrome, and instead of falling into the "if God were on my side, this wouldn't be happening" syndrome, we need to focus on the aspects of our circumstances that can demonstrate the attributes of God. We need to embrace this perspective that places highest priority on the revelation of his nature.

Not only is that practical, and not only does it fit the premise of this book, but it's also biblically mandated. When we find ourselves in a seemingly hopeless situation, we are urged by Scripture to display the hope that has been birthed within us. When we find ourselves in a long, intractable difficulty, we are told to demonstrate patience in the same way that God demonstrated his patience with us. When we find ourselves in an unfair situation, we are commanded to demonstrate the forgiving nature of God. When evil assaults, we can resist it with the righteousness God has displayed and given to us. And when others think all hope is lost, we are to be an example, looking forward either to an impending miracle or an end-of-time redemption of all that seems tragic in our lives. All of these responses are more than good, scriptural advice; they are strong urgings of the inspired Word.

Like many biblical commands, these responses are not easy. When tragedy strikes or evil threatens, our default setting is to look inside ourselves and focus on the impact on our own lives. What God calls us to do through the repeated urgings of Scripture is to look to him for a way to demonstrate his character. Revelation, both in terms of biblical inspiration and in how God comes to us today, is not just information God gives us for instruction; it never has been, not from Genesis 1 through Revelation 22 and not in his present work in our lives. Our trials are part of the tragic story of human history, but in them we have been given the high honor of becoming participants in his demonstration of himself to this world. And the best way to do that on a broken, rebellious planet is to display his very character in the midst of the brokenness—even when that brokenness painfully involves us.

Consider all the possibilities of what that means. We've mentioned a few in the paragraphs above, but they may not have hit home for you. Make it personal now. What trial are you going through that you could apply this principle to? What would this desire for divine revelation look like to a man whose wife has deserted him or to a woman whose husband has betrayed her? Would it involve a zealous pursuit of reconciliation? An astoundingly generous forgiveness? A dramatic miracle that redeems the situation immediately? A firm stand against unholiness? The possibilities are limited only by the character of God himself.

What would it look like to a mother and father who have lost their son to cancer, or to a car accident, or to some other tragic death? Would it involve fixing their gaze on the hope of the resurrection? A patient, persistent trust in God's promise that he will make all things new and redeem all of our pain? An astoundingly generous forgiveness of whomever, if anyone, was at fault? Again the possibilities are limited only by the character of God.

Let's take the scenario most often referred to in the discussion of pain and evil: the Holocaust. What does the Godward view look like in such a devastating, seemingly senseless tragedy? How can God possibly be displayed when children have watched their parents die at the hands of cruel, wicked men or when parents have seen their children tortured? Is there any way to look heavenward and hope for the display of a merciful God? The situation almost seems to indict him, not glorify him. How can he be revealed in such darkness?

Perhaps the darkness is the best place for him to be revealed. Millions of lives have been changed by the stories of Corrie ten Boom and her sister Betsie—their time in prison and in a labor camp, and God's protection of them even when their circumstances were dreadful. Their Bible teaching changed lives in prison, and their story has changed lives in the decades since. But how many people would have heard of Corrie ten Boom—how many would have known the power and love of the God she serves—if she had not been through the horrors of a concentration camp? She had a viable ministry before the war; she had greater impact during and after it. God was there in the darkness, and though some people see only the darkness, others couldn't have seen the light without her. She had a choice—shine light in the darkness or let her spirit be extinguished in it. She saw the light of God and shined it for others to see.

It's hard to understand how anyone could see God in the Holocaust, but many people like Corrie did. They chose to do so because they believed the light of God could pierce the darkest of worlds. The invisible attributes of God may have become only faintly visible at first, but minimal amounts of biblically based faith made them grow more and more concrete. The Holocaust is not the ultimate argument against God. Though millions were killed in that event, no one who trusted his eternal salvation died in the truest sense of the word. That speaks volumes about the nature of God.

And that's our calling, isn't it? To speak volumes about the nature of God. We've been put in a peculiar position, and an exceedingly painful one at that. Those who choose to believe the once hidden attributes of God, however, will experience them in spite of the pain. And in our faith, we become his most powerful demonstration to a universe that had never seen unmerited grace or miraculous restoration. The faith of his people says volumes about who God is. The world suffers, and he is revealed in the suffering—ours, personally and specifically—if we will make his revelation our holy pursuit.

The promise of God as he has revealed himself in the Bible is that this earth experience is all going somewhere. There is a purpose to the pain. This world is not the result of a God who wishes we had not fallen in the garden and is now scrambling to come up with the best redemption plan possible. He is not just making lemonade out of his creation's lemons. There was a point to it all from the very beginning—according to Scripture, we were chosen for redemption before the foundation of the world. It was designed from day one. Even if the outer darkness is full of lamented, discarded material, the heavenly scene will be full of beautiful sculptures—images of the sacred, refined and polished in pain. The glory of God will come out ahead of all its rivals.

17

One Day Looking Back

No eye has seen, nor ear heard, nor the heart of man imagined, what God has prepared for those who love him.

1 Corinthians 2:9

If you've suffered, you've probably grown suspicious of certain biblical promises. Consider the following:

> When the righteous cry for help, the LORD hears and delivers them out of all their troubles. The LORD is near to the brokenhearted and saves the crushed in spirit. Many are the afflictions of the righteous, but the LORD delivers him out of them all.
>
> Psalm 34:17–19

> Bless the LORD, O my soul, and forget not all his benefits, who forgives all your iniquity, who heals all your diseases, who redeems your life from the pit, who crowns you with steadfast love and mercy, who satisfies you with good so that your youth is renewed like the eagle's.
>
> Psalm 103:2–5

You don't completely believe that, do you? Experience compels us to water these promises down somehow. We know of instances when God did not deliver us from all our troubles or heal all our diseases. No, we're a little more likely to embrace Paul's assessment—that God comforts us in all our afflictions (2 Cor. 1:4). That's a promise we can handle.

What happened between the psalms and Paul? Why is it that God was known to be the Deliverer from all troubles in the Old Testament and the Comforter in the midst of them in the New?

It's a false tension. There is no contradiction, nor is there a watering down of the promises. God also comforted in the Old Testament, and he also delivered in the New. The promises of the whole Scripture are all true. God will deliver the righteous out of all their troubles, and he will deliver them from all their diseases and redeem their lives from the pit. "Though the Lord give you the bread of adversity and water of affliction, yet your Teacher will not hide himself anymore, but your eyes shall see your Teacher" (Isa. 30:20). The problem is the time lapse between the promise and the fulfillment. We expect the promises of these psalms above, for example, to be fulfilled immediately. Sometimes they are; sometimes they are not. We forget that any healing or deliverance God offers now isn't permanent anyway; we will all get sick and die. And the healing or deliverance he promises in the kingdom isn't immediate for most of us. We want immediate *and* permanent, and we can't have both, not in this age. Somewhere between them we begin to question God.

What is our solution to that? It is to be completely preoccupied with the glory to come. Numerous passages of Scripture tell us to do so. The author of Hebrews tells us to fix our eyes on Jesus (12:2). Peter tells us, "Rejoice insofar as you share Christ's sufferings, that you may also rejoice and be glad when his glory is revealed" (1 Pet. 4:13). Paul tells us to run the race with an eye on the prize (1 Cor. 9:27).

More Than a Feeling

Is this just a good psychological trick to distract us from our pain—a sort of spiritual anesthesia? Is religion really the opiate of the masses, turning our apathetic heads toward eternity while we ignore issues closer to home? Or can we legitimately say, with Paul, that "to live is Christ, and to die is gain" (Phil. 1:21)?

We might struggle with the idea of a God who uses his people in a painful way to demonstrate his own character for his own glory, but only when we see God as a human being like us. We forget the lavish promises of his Word. Consider what's in store for us:

- Jesus has betrothed his followers; we are his eternal bride (Revelation 21).
- We will see him face-to-face (1 Cor. 13:12).
- We are being transformed into his likeness with ever-increasing glory (2 Cor. 3:18).
- He will transform our earthly bodies to be like his incorruptible, resurrected body (Phil. 3:21).
- We will feast forever in his kingdom (Matt. 8:11; Luke 14:15; Rev. 19:9).
- "There shall no longer be any mourning, or crying, or pain; *the first things have passed away. . . . Behold, I am making all things new*" (Rev. 21:4–5 NASB).

Those are life-giving words for those whose eyes are rubbed raw from grief in this world. This God who has allowed our pain as a platform for his glory is by no means selfish. He offers to live with us in intimate, divine, wedded bliss forever. It is a union that will know no tear, no complaint, no distress, no grief.

Many are familiar with the story of the five missionaries who died at the hands of the Auca Indians in Ecuador in 1956. They had invested their lives in reaching an unreached tribe, and they had planned out their ministry well. Contact had already been made and gifts already exchanged by low-flying aircraft. Everything pointed to a safe first landing and the beginning of a fruitful relationship. So when that time came, the missionaries set out for the fulfillment of their mission. They were never heard from again and were later found floating in the river with spears through them. Elisabeth Elliot, widow of one of the missionaries, has written beautifully about the worthiness of the cause and the fruit of the sacrifice.

Many are familiar with the story of Joni Eareckson Tada, who was paralyzed in an accident as a teenager and spent years struggling with and coming to terms with her infirmity. She held out hope for physical healing in the first years after her injury, but God chose to bless her with a different miracle. Her testimony is a marvel of endurance and grace.

There are numerous examples of people who have suffered and in whom God has glorified himself. They are part of the panorama of God's intervention in this lost world. They are witnesses to all that the Bible says about our pain. It can always be redeemed, and it will live on in memories as an eternal testimony to grace.

Paul is explicit in Romans 8: if we suffer with Christ, we will be glorified with him (v. 17). The glory to be revealed is not just God's. By nature of his generosity, it is ours as well. We have been set free from corruption to be free in our glory as children of God (v. 21). It is of "eternal weight" and far "beyond all comparison" (2 Cor. 4:17). No one can yet comprehend it—whatever we can imagine, the honor he will share with us is greater. God will not end up owing anyone anything. If we believe his promise on his terms, whatever we have spent in suffering will be more than compensated for in blessing.

But in the midst of suffering, it's hard for the weight of glory to overshadow the weight of grief. We can be told how light our momentary affliction is, but it seems so heavy. We see the pain. We only hear of the future promise. And that's the problem. Somehow we have to get perspective on the brokenness of our lives. We have to imagine ourselves looking back on it. We must see ourselves standing in eternity, glancing backward at the grief and knowing it is past. We know it is temporary; we must see just how temporary it is. We will echo the bold response of all who have suffered hard things before us and maintained their faith: "I would never choose to go through it again, but I'm glad for what God did in it."

How can we see this? With the eyes of faith. Either all of these promises of future redemption of our pain are true, or they are hogwash. We cannot look at them as our backup plan in case things don't soon take a turn for the better. We must plant both feet in eternity and know that the comfort there is infinitely greater than the discomfort now. We must see with the eyes of the New Testament Christians who did not love their lives "even unto death" (Rev. 12:11).

That's how we overcome, whether it's in the area of sin and guilt, temptation, or suffering; we embrace a wholesale rejection of our stake in the here-and-now life, knowing the value of the kingdom of God. It doesn't mean we won't feel pain; it means pain won't do us in. We will overcome it, because we have a promise from the Overcomer.

Lyrics for a New Song

> They sang a new song.
>
> Revelation 5:9

> They were singing a new song before the throne and before the four living creatures and before the elders.
>
> Revelation 14:3

We're given glimpses of God throughout the Bible. The language is always sketchy and figurative—wheels within wheels, jasper and sardius, crystal expanses and radiance—because our languages simply cannot describe the utter transcendence, infinity, and otherness of God. He is someone to behold but never to fully grasp. We are only given glimpses, because glimpses are all we humans can see. No one can behold the wholeness of God. We just aren't capable.

But we are given these amazing glimpses. Isaiah saw one: "Holy, holy, holy is the LORD of hosts," the seraphim would call out to one another (Isa. 6:3). Ezekiel saw one: flashing fire, burning coals, clouds of mystery, eyes everywhere, and strange wheels. Daniel saw one: a river of fire and the Ancient of Days. John saw one: eyes of flame, a voice like rushing waters, a crystal sea. And Moses saw one: a descending cloud and a voice saying, "The LORD, the LORD, a God merciful and gracious, slow to anger, and abounding in steadfast love and faithfulness" (Exod. 34:6). None of these beholders of glory would be the same afterward. To encounter God is to be forever changed.

The faith hall of fame found in Hebrews 11 lists mighty men and women who fixed their gaze on these eternal glimpses. Abraham looked for "the city that has foundations, whose designer and builder is God" (v. 10). Moses considered "the reproach of Christ greater wealth than the treasures of Egypt, for he was looking to the reward" (v. 26). These heroes of faith wandered in deserts and mountains, lived in caves, suffered violence and contempt, all because they saw a future glory. They died without receiving the promise—yet.

The pain of the scars of men and women do not compare to the comfort of the healing touch of God—not in the long run. Jesus became our eternal example of one who looked past shame and endured torture "for the joy that was set before him" (Heb. 12:2). This is the norm for us: we know we must endure pain before getting to heaven. But I've suggested in this book that for the rest of creation, that is not the norm. The broken context of this world has revealed things about God that could not have been revealed any other way. This story of Eden/fall/deliverance/eternal joy has demonstrated something about God that was once hidden in eternity past. Angels—cherubim, seraphim, strange beings with wheels and wings—and, in addition, fallen angels—principalities, powers, rulers of this present darkness—did not know everything there was to know about God. No one ever does, of course. But the earth event has shown him off in some very dramatic ways.

I love reading about all the glimpses of God in the Bible, and I have a theory. It's sort of a theory of evolution—the evolution of praise. It's a two-part, no-brainer of a theory: (1) praise expands as God reveals more and more of himself to his creatures, and (2) there is something entirely and profoundly unique about his revelation of himself in the human drama. I believe that heaven once resounded with sounds of majesty and splendor: the "holy, holy, holy" of the seraphim; the flashes of lightning and fire; the "worthy are you, our Lord and God, to receive glory and honor and power" (Rev. 4:11); and a multitude of worshipful sounds extolling the greatness of the powerful, majestic, glorious God. I believe those sounds are still resounding in the heavenly places, but I believe there are new sounds. They are sounds that spring from God's involvement with one broken, long-suffering planet.

The book of Revelation is a glorious book. Read the praises of the angels and elders and the redeemed sometime. There is overwhelming ecstasy in the shouts and songs of worship. But do you notice something about Revelation's praise? After all this sin and brokenness business is over, there are shouts of triumph and righteous judgment as the dragon is doomed and Babylon is laid waste. There are songs of salvation and grace. There are hints of new songs being sung: "Worthy are you to take the scroll and to open its seals, for you were slain, and by your blood you ransomed people for God" (5:9); and "No one could learn that song except for the 144,000 who had been redeemed" (14:3). There are songs from our history of brokenness being sung, like the Song of Moses—a joyful celebration of deliverance that first rang out in Exodus 15—and the Song of the Lamb: "Great and amazing are your deeds . . . for your righteous acts have been revealed" (Rev. 15:3). These songs extol the glory of the rescuer God. Amazing attributes of the Lord have been revealed. Salvation has been demonstrated. Evil has been forever defeated. *Mercy has come!*

Don't let that observation go by too quickly. Whenever the final book of the Bible mentions a new song, the content has to do with compassion and salvation and grace. Such praises are, in the eternal scheme of things, apparently a novelty. Who would have sung them before this whole earth catastrophe was set in motion? On what occasion would seraphim have blessed God with such praises of grace and deliverance if there were no fall? What perfect heaven would have displayed this side of his glory? What pure context could have shown his manifold mercies in the way this broken planet has? What prehumanity song could speak of his marvelous work of salvation?

The answer to all of these questions should be clear by now. If God were to set the stage to reveal himself as merciful Deliverer, Healer, Savior, Warrior, Refuge, and so on, as we have seen, this is exactly the kind of creation we would expect to find: a fallen one, a creation in need of deliverance, healing, redemption, victory, and protection. In Revelation the sad story of our fallen world ends with a "happily ever after." The suffering and pain were temporary thorns in God's kingdom. The full array of the attributes of God is clearly visible. And we are his beneficiaries, the eternal display of those attributes, the case in point for all his mercies, the testimony for all who care to see.

The mystery is profound, and its revelation may take an eternity to grasp. The ravages of this fallen planet inflicted scars on the Son of God. It has inflicted scars on all of us, but his are the worst. His scars absorb the brunt of the pain on our behalf. And they are eternal. Jesus ascended with them, and he lives with them now. The temporal has marred the Eternal One. But the glory is eternal too. The scars are the eternal reminder of God's character—that once there was a planet in rebellion, and the powerful, majestic, almighty God showed his merciful side, saving and delivering and healing. The hands and the feet of Jesus are forever held up as the example of the once hidden mercies of God. According to Ephesians 2:7, he is for display. His wounds are the everlasting testimony: this is what God is like.

Yes, the King of heaven is now also King of the nations (Rev. 15:3). Sinful man has been made pure by a righteous Redeemer (15:4). The harlot is judged and the bride is made ready (Rev. 19:2, 7). The celebration has begun, and he, the Revealed One, shall reign forever and ever.

Your Stage Is Set

Your life, whether you like it or not, is a stage. You are not the star performer; God is. The opening act of this play was tragic. The middle acts sometimes foreshadow the wonderful finale, but they are often painful, confusing, and just hanging there. Most of the audience is wondering what the point of this play is. But the final act will make it all clear. All things will be resolved. The star performer will be vindicated. He is already receiving applause from some quarters of the audience—those who get it. The rest of them will break out into a spontaneous ovation once they get it too. Everyone—the audience, the other actors, the distant observers, the critics, the stagehands, everyone—will be amazed. God will take a bow, and everyone will see sides of him they had never even thought of before.

And, yes, there is a promise: it will definitely be worth the price of admission.

Notes

Chapter 1: Something's Wrong

1. John Stott, *The Cross of Christ* (Downers Grove, IL: InterVarsity Press, 1986), 311.

2. Lee Strobel, *The Case for Faith* (Grand Rapids: Zondervan, 2000).

3. Epicurus, quoted in Strobel, *The Case for Faith*, 25.

4. Elwood McQuaid, *The Zion Connection* (Eugene, OR: Harvest House, 1996), 48–49.

Chapter 6: The Centerpiece of the Universe

1. John Piper, *Desiring God* (Portland: Multnomah, 1996), 43.

2. Ibid., 355.

3. For better and deeper explanations of the God-centeredness of God, see Piper's *Desiring God*; *The Pleasures of God* (Portland: Multnomah, 1991); and *God's Passion for His Glory: Living the Vision of Jonathan Edwards* (Wheaton: Crossway, 1998).

Chapter 9: In the Eyes of Angels

1. We don't know why mercy isn't applied to the devil and his fellow rebels, but the leading theory seems to be that as beings with a clear vision of the Almighty, their rebellion was calculated, decisive, and final. Ours was rebellion also, but we inherited corruption from our first parents and were first enslaved to sin in ignorance. Any further discussion of this is simply speculation, however. The Bible just doesn't tell us why God's redemption seems to be a phenomenon primarily among humans.

Chapter 10: Eternity in Their Eyes

1. Rodney Stark, *The Rise of Christianity* (New York: HarperCollins, 1997), 164–65.

2. Piper, *Desiring God*, 40.

Chapter 11: What Kind of Love?

1. No, I'm not implying that our benefit and his might contradict. What benefits him benefits those who love him. The two purposes are completely complementary. His glory equals our good—as long as we aren't rebelling against it and seeking our own glory.

2. I would again point the reader to John Piper's *Desiring God*, *The Pleasures of God*, and *God's Passion for His Glory* for better and deeper explanations of the God-centeredness of God.

3. It is beyond coincidence that two people who suffered greatly in the Old Testament, Job and Joseph, both consider themselves doubly blessed in the end. Job saw that blessing quite literally, with twice the amount of visible prosperity. And Joseph named one of his children Ephraim ("twice fruitful"), because, as Genesis 41:52 quotes him, "God has made me fruitful in the land of my affliction."

Chapter 13: When All Hell Breaks Loose

1. The literal translation of the Greek in Matthew 6:13 supports "evil one" rather than the commonly used "evil."

Chapter 15: Spiritual Street Children

1. C. S. Lewis, *The Problem of Pain* (New York: Simon and Schuster, 1996), 83.

Chris Tiegreen is the editor of *indeed* magazine, a deeper-life devotional published by Walk Thru the Bible, and author of *At His Feet* and *The One Year Walk with God Devotional.* He and his family live in Atlanta, Georgia.